Meditation on the Nature of Mind

Meditation on the Nature of Mind

Tenzin Gyatso
The Fourteenth Dalai Lama

Khöntön Peljor Lhündrub

&

José Ignacio Cabezón

Wisdom Publications • Boston

Wisdom Publications
199 Elm Street
Somerville MA 02144 USA
www.wisdompubs.org

Library of Congress Cataloging-in-Publication Data
Bstan-'dzin-rgya-mtsho, Dalai Lama XIV, 1935–
 Meditation on the nature of mind / Tenzin Gyatso, the Fourteenth Dalai Lama, Khöntön Peljor Lhündrub & José Ignacio Cabezón.
  p. cm.
 Includes translation of The wish-fulfilling jewel of the oral tradition.
 Includes bibliographical references and index.
 ISBN 0-86171-628-0 (pbk. : alk. paper)
 1. Consciousness—Religious aspects—Buddhism. 2. Meditation—Buddhism. 3. Buddhism—Doctrines. 4. 'Khon-ston Dpal-'byor Lhun-grub, 1561–1637. I. Cabezón, José Ignacio, 1956– II. 'Khon-ston Dpal-'byor Lhun-grub, 1561–1637. Sñan rgyud yid bzin nor bu lta ba spyi khyab tu no sprod pa'i khrid yig. English. III. Title.
 BQ7935.B774M43 2011
 294.3'442—dc22

                         2011007536

 ISBN 978-0-86171-628-9
 eBook ISBN: 978-0-86171-629-6

15 14 13 12 11
5   4   3   2   1

Cover design by Rick Snizik. Interior design by Gopa&Ted2. Set in Centaur 12/16. Photographs on pages ii, ix, and 2 by Tony Mastres and Randall Lamb (USCB Photo).

Wisdom Publications' books are printed on acid-free paper and meet the guidelines for permanence and durability of the Production Guidelines for Book Longevity of the Council on Library Resources.

Printed in the United States of America.

This book was produced with environmental mindfulness. We have elected to print this title on 30% PCW recycled paper. As a result, we have saved the following resources: 26 trees, 8 million BTUs of energy, 2,457 lbs. of greenhouse gases, 11,834 gallons of water, and 718 lbs. of solid waste. For more information, please visit our website, www.wisdompubs.org. This paper is also FSC certified. For more information, please visit www.fscus.org.

Contents

Preface

IN 2007, while reading through a collection of Tibetan texts published two years earlier in eastern Tibet, I came across a short meditation text on the nature of mind, *The Wish-Fulfilling Jewel of the Oral Tradition*, written by the Tibetan scholar Khöntön Peljor Lhündrub (1561–1637), or Khöntönpa. The work piqued my interest for a number of reasons: clearly written, it manages to combine both theory and practical instructions for meditating on the nature of mind in a manner that is easily accessible. Especially interesting was the nonsectarian approach it took in regard to its subject matter, with liberal citations of scholars from across the Tibetan Buddhist spectrum. One other thing made the text intriguing to me personally: it was written by the fifteenth abbot of Sera Monastery's Jé College, at which I had lived and studied as a monk for six years in the 1980s.

In the summer of 2008, I briefly met His Holiness the Dalai Lama during his visit to Pennsylvania, and as the organizer for his upcoming visit to the University of California Santa Barbara, I requested him to lecture on Khöntön Rinpoché's text. His Holiness replied that he knew the text, but that his schedule did not permit him to give a detailed commentary on the work. Instead, he agreed to offer some general remarks that would contextualize Khöntönpa's text within the broader field of Indo-Tibetan Buddhist thought. This became the subject of His Holiness's first lecture at UCSB on the morning of April 24, 2009, a lecture entitled "The Nature of Mind." His Holiness's broad-ranging overview of this important topic constitutes the first part of this book. The lecture insightfully distills some of the most central themes of Buddhism: why the mind is so essential to the tradition, how science and traditional Buddhist learning can benefit from mutual interaction, what distinguishes subtle and grosser levels of consciousness, how the different schools of Tibetan Buddhism elaborate such a distinction, and how all of these schools have a common source in the scholarly tradition of Nalanda Monastery, the greatest Buddhist university of ancient India. His Holiness's teaching was profound and erudite, both in scope and detail, and I am grateful to him for allowing its publication in this book.

The rest of this volume is devoted to Khöntön Peljor Lhündrub and to what is arguably his most important extant work, *The Wish-Fulfilling Jewel*. As little has been written in Western languages about Khöntön Rinpoché, I have composed a short biography of this interesting figure. The biography is based on the few Tibetan sources on Khöntön Rinpoché's life available to us, chiefly the biography written by his most famous student, the Fifth Dalai Lama. An annotated translation of *The Wish-Fulfilling Jewel* follows the biography. I have tried to make the translation as accessible as possible, rendering Tibetan names and terms in phonetics (rather than in the more difficult Wylie transliteration scheme) and avoiding the use of Sanskrit diacritical marks in the main body of the translation. Full Wylie transliteration, references to the Indian and Tibetan sources cited by Khöntönpa, and discussions of a more scholarly nature have been relegated to the notes.

His Holiness the Dalai Lama's 2009 visit to the campus of the University of California Santa Barbara was his fourth visit here, and the first since an endowed professorship—the XIVth Dalai Lama Chair of Tibetan Buddhism and Cultural Studies—was established in his honor. His Holiness gave two public lectures to sold-out audiences, with five thousand people at each event. This was an extraordinary opportunity for students, faculty, and members of the Santa Barbara and surrounding communities to listen to and learn from one of the great religious thinkers of our time.

His Holiness the Dalai Lama at UC Santa Barbara

In the months prior to His Holiness's visit, a wide variety of programs were organized on campus to celebrate Tibetan culture. The university libraries selected His Holiness's *Ethics for a New Millennium* as its choice for the annual UCSB Reads program. Two thousand copies of the book were made available at no cost to students, staff, and faculty. Forums on the book were also held throughout Santa Barbara. In addition to the ongoing courses on Tibetan Buddhism and Tibetan language offered in the Religious Studies Department, other classes on Tibetan-Himalayan anthropology and Tibetan medicine were taught in the Department of East Asian Languages and Cultural Studies. In early spring, the prime minister of the Tibetan government in exile, Ven. Professor Samdhong Rinpoche, gave a lecture on "The Future of Tibet." A few weeks later, Pico Iyer and Professor Robert Thurman engaged in a public conversation on "Why the Dalai Lama Matters" at UCSB's Campbell Hall. Members of the UC Santa Barbara faculty also lectured on Tibetan culture and religion in the local community, and the University Art Museum organized an extraordinary exhibition, "Toward Enlightenment: The Sacred Art of Tibet," showcasing exquisite *tangka* paintings from the collection of the Rubin Museum of Art. In the weeks prior to His Holiness's visit, a renowned monk-artist from Gyümé Tantric College taught a month-long workshop on Tibetan painting for undergraduates; and in the days before His Holiness's arrival, monks from Drepung Loseling Monastery created a beautiful Avalokiteshvara sand-mandala in honor of the Dalai Lama. In the words of Dean David Marshall, "This remarkable program of events culminating in the Dalai Lama's lectures was, for our students and the wider community, an example of our public university at its very best."

The planning of these various events, including the visit of His Holiness, involved dozens of individuals from across the campus. I would like to take this opportunity to thank all of my university colleagues for their selfless and devoted work, and Chancellor Henry Yang and Dean David Marshall for their unstinting support and encouragement. I would also like to express my gratitude to the staff of the Office of Tibet in New York, and especially to Mr. Lobsang Nyandak, the Dalai Lama's chief representative. Heartfelt thanks as well to Dr. Thupten Jinpa, His Holiness's most able interpreter, for serving as translator.

For their help with the preparation of the manuscript, I wish to thank Nathaniel Rich, Greg Seton, and Nathan McGovern. In addition, I would like to express my gratitude to Geshe Dorji Damdul for his helpful suggestions on the book as a whole and to Mr. David Kittelstrom of Wisdom Publications for his insightful observations and keen editorial eye.

Finally, as the organizer of the Dalai Lama's visit to the University of California Santa Barbara in 2009, I would like to thank His Holiness for gracing us with his presence and for his inspiring teachings. I also wish to add my voice to the numerous individuals around the world who pray for His Holiness's health, long life, and the fulfillment of all his wishes.

རྒྱལ་བའི་ལུང་རྟོགས་བསྟན་པར་མཁའ་བརྟེས་པ།
ནུ་ལན་དུ་ཡི་བཀའ་སློ་འཛིན་པའི་གཙོ།
རྒྱུ་བོད་རིས་མེད་ལུགས་ཀྱི་མཁའ་བདག་རྗེ།
ཆོས་ཀྱི་རྒྱ་མཚོ་ཐབས་ལ་མཁས་པ་ཅན།

འཇམ་གླིང་མགོན་པོ་བསྐུན་འཛིན་རྒྱ་མཚོ་མཆོག།
ང་འདྲ་སྨྲ་བས་ཚིག་རྣམས་ལ་ཕུལ་ཏེས་གཟིགས།
འཁོར་བ་མ་སྟོགས་བར་དུ་བརྟན་བཞུགས་ནས།
འཆི་མེད་ཆོས་ཀྱི་འཁོར་ལོ་སྐོར་དུ་གསོལ།

José Ignacio Cabezón
XIVth Dalai Lama Professor
University of California Santa Barbara
June 2009

The Nature of Mind

His Holiness the Dalai Lama

SINCE MY REMARKS today are mainly based on the texts of the Buddhist tradition, I want to begin with a verse of salutation to the Buddha composed by the Indian master Nagarjuna.

> Homage to Gautama,
> who, out of his compassion and mercy,
> taught the holy doctrine
> so as to eliminate all wrong views.

My brothers and sisters—and when I say "brothers and sisters," I really mean it! Especially at this moment in our history, we are in real need of such a warmhearted spirit. Our usual concept of "us" and "them" is outdated. In its place, we need an attitude that sees all human beings as our brothers and sisters, that considers others to be part of "us." Most of the problems that we confront day to day are essentially man-made. They are unnecessary. The natural problems of life are quite enough, so what point is there in creating additional problems for ourselves? Is this wise? Certainly not. All these man-made problems ultimately derive from dividing the world in this way: "us" versus "them." We think to ourselves, "We matter; they don't." As a result, we disregard the welfare of others, at times even exploiting and cheating them. That is why I always emphasize the need for a sense of global responsibility. It is foolish to think that the interests of six billion human beings are less important than one's own. Every one of us yearns for a happy life. No one deliberately works to create problems or suffering; each of us acts with the intention to bring about happier days. But because we focus on ourselves alone, caring little about others—because we operate out of an egoistic motivation—our actions become unrealistic. We act improperly, and as a result, all kinds of unwanted problems arise, created by ourselves alone. We therefore need a healthy and proper mental attitude. I think this is very important.

By now humanity has paid adequate attention to material development. Compare our preoccupation with our material well-being with the attention we pay to our minds. Our concern with inner development and inner values pales by comparison, doesn't it? Science and technology have brought us a multitude of material advances in the twentieth century; these advances have sometimes also brought us greater fear and anxiety. Today, at the outset of the twenty-first century, we must ask ourselves: Why have these material advances, which are meant to improve the lives of human beings, failed to bring us greater contentment? Happiness and joy are mental states, feelings. The same is true of sadness and pain. These are all states of mind. And yet, we neglect the mind. Because pain and pleasure are mental states, if we do not pay attention to our minds, then no matter how intent we may be to obtain pleasure and reduce pain, we will not succeed.

I have noticed over the years that some of my wealthier friends are among the most unhappy people I know. It is true that the rich often have more friends—although whether these friends are friends of the wealthy or of their wealth is a different question! In any case,

I have seen that even with their many friends, a wealthy person may be profoundly unhappy. The search for comfort in money and power is wrongheaded and simply does not work. The more effective way of dealing with our unhappiness is to pay attention to inner values, to the inner sciences of the mind. What do you think?

Studying the Mind

All major religious traditions agree about one message: the message of love and compassion, the spirit of forgiveness and tolerance. With an awareness that negative actions bring about negative consequences, the major religions also teach us to practice self-discipline. The practice of self-discipline brings us greater contentment—even someone with a strictly materialist perspective can recognize this. These basic ethical guidelines and the teaching to love one's neighbor are found in all traditions.

Loving kindness and compassion are mental qualities. By training in them, we try to reduce anger, hatred, fear, and suspicion—negative, destructive emotions that are also a part of the mind. These two things—the positive mental attitudes that bring us joy and the destructive emotions that lead to pain—are things we experience with our minds. All the major religions teach us that we should practice a method to improve our minds. In this regard, they are the same.

There are also differences between religious traditions, of course. Some religions are theistic, others nontheistic. Theistic religions emphasize the importance of faith in a creator God. Note that faith is also a mental state, or experience. That is the basic approach of theism. Nontheistic religions such as Jainism, Buddhism, and a subschool of the ancient Indian Samkhya tradition propound something like "self-creation" based on the law of causality: cause and effect. Nontheistic religions ultimately believe that we ourselves are the creator. Naturally, this creator cannot be the body. The body is important as the basis of mind: for example, the human body is the basis of human mind, and we distinguish different types of sentient beings—animals and so on—on the basis of their different bodies. And sensory consciousnesses are entirely based on physiology. But ultimately, physical actions and speech—that is, verbal actions—are driven by motivations. And when we are dealing with motivations, we are of course dealing with a nonsensory level of mind. According to the law of causality, everything that we experience—whether pleasant or unpleasant—is ultimately linked to our motivation, to our minds. Thus, in order to live a happy and joyful life, we have to take care of our minds; we have to cultivate the right types of motivation. In order to reduce or to overcome suffering, we have to deal with our negative or destructive emotions, the ultimate causes of unwanted consequences, like pain. For this reason, nontheistic traditions place special emphasis on the mind.

Naturally, logically, to effectively deal with the mind, we must have a thorough knowledge of what the mind is. This thing we call "mind" or "consciousness" is very complex. There are many different types of mental events that constitute it: thousands upon thousands. Many of these are destructive emotions. The only way to deal with these destructive emotions is through the mind itself—not through wealth, or injections, or surgery, but only through mental measures. Drugs and alcohol cannot reduce anger or hatred. True, sometimes when we are experiencing a great deal of inner turmoil, like anger, a pill may help us to sleep, and the next morning the anger is slightly weaker. But basically, the only way to effectively deal with negative or destructive emotions, the only way to really reduce them, is through the mind, through the application of counteractive mental states that oppose the negative emotions affecting us. First, we must understand the counteractive agent, or antidote, to be applied, and then we need to slowly increase its power. That is the only real, long-term way to reduce negative emotions. Another way of saying it is that to effectively reduce destructive emotions we need to increase the power of constructive emotions. But again, this requires that we understand the mind—that we have the ability to discern which thoughts are ultimately destructive and which are ultimately constructive.

This brings us to a big question: Is it even possible to eliminate destructive emotions? In order to answer that question we have to know what is the ultimate nature of mind—what is the basis of all these destructive emotions. For we can only determine the possibility of eliminating destructive emotions by gaining some sense of the mind's true nature. That is why the Buddhist texts contain so much information about the emotions and about the mind generally.

LEVELS OF MIND

The tantras explain methods of manipulating the subtle physiology of the body—the channels, energies, and drops that parallel our gross nervous system. These tantric techniques are the means that allow practitioners access to successively more subtle levels of mind. This discussion is explicitly found *only* in the tantric texts. For example, at this very moment, it is our sensory consciousness that is fully functioning, that is most active. While our senses—our sight, hearing, and so on—are operating, thoughts are also flowing, but sensory consciousness dominates during the ordinary waking state. When we dream, however, sensory consciousness no longer functions; only thought—another, more subtle level of mind—operates during the dream state. Then, during deep sleep, sleep without dreaming, there is another, deeper level of consciousness or mind that operates. And when someone faints, at which point even the breath may stop, another, still deeper level of mind is experienced. Finally, at the time of death, all physiological processes cease in an instant: the heart stops beating, the blood stops circulating in the brain, and so forth. The neurons then cease to function, and with the cessation of the body's grosser physical functioning, all grosser levels of mind come to a halt as well. What we ordinarily know as the human mind is no longer active. It stops. The only indication that a more subtle level of mind is still present is the fact that the bodies of some individuals remain fresh even after they have been declared clinically dead.

Let me give you some examples. The physical body of my own senior tutor remained very fresh, in the way just mentioned, even after he had been dead for thirteen days. And about a year or so ago, the body of another senior Tibetan lama, the former throne-holder of Ganden, remained fresh for almost three weeks after he had died. As soon as I heard that this master's body was remaining in this naturally fresh state, I asked a medical center in Dharamsala, the village in northern India where I live, to carry out an investigation. This medical center had a simple machine for measuring brain activity. They sent a team with the machine and placed electrodes on the lama's head. Although a very detailed analysis of the results of these tests has yet to be completed, it seems that even a few days after he had been declared clinically dead, some very weak electrical signals could be detected in this lama's brain. This, I was told, is very unusual. We believe that these findings indicate that the lama's innermost subtle mind was still present and having some measurable influence on the body. This state of mind—the mind that is present at the time of death—is what we call the *most subtle consciousness*. In any case, the broader point is that there are many levels of mind.

The *Abhidharmakosha*, or *Treasury of Knowledge*, written by the fourth-century Indian Buddhist master Vasubandhu, explains how various moments of consciousness give rise to one another: how, for example, there can be transitions from virtuous states of mind to neutral ones, then to nonvirtuous ones, and so forth. Vasubandhu speaks about the death process in the context of this discussion. He explains that at the moment of death, consciousness can be virtuous, nonvirtuous, or neutral depending upon the individual and his or her particular situation. However, the *Abhidharmasamuccaya*, or *Compendium of Knowledge*, written by Vasubandhu's half-brother Asanga, explains that the subtle consciousness at the time of death is neither virtuous nor nonvirtuous but instead neutral. This suggests that Asanga considers the subtle consciousness at the moment of death to be more subtle. He explains that while the rougher levels of consciousness can be either virtuous or nonvirtuous, the more subtle level of consciousness at the time of death can be neither virtuous nor nonvirtuous and can only be neutral.

The tantric texts explain that through the practice of inner yoga, through meditation, one can transform that subtlest consciousness at the moment of death from a neutral state into a virtuous one, but that the subtlemost level of mind can never change into a non-virtuous mental state. The point here is that nonvirtuous states of mind can only operate during the time that the "eighty types of conceptual thoughts," the grosser levels of consciousness, are operating. As the mind shuts down, the eighty types of conceptual thoughts cease, and through a process known as the *four emptinesses,* the most subtle mind manifests. Nonvirtuous thoughts cease at this stage. This means that nonvirtuous mental states are only found when the grosser levels of consciousness are active. Nonetheless, the most subtle level of consciousness, also known as the *primordial innate mind,* can be *transformed* from a neutral into a virtuous state of mind. Notice this difference: using the special methods of tantra, the most subtle level of mind can be transformed into a virtuous state, but the subtlest mind can never change into a nonvirtuous mental state.

BASIS, PATH, AND RESULT

For the reasons just explained, in order to gain a complete under-standing of the mind, it is necessary to include the perspective of the tantric texts, of the Vajrayana. In one of the most important such texts, the *Guhyasamaja Tantra,* there is an explanation of the meaning of the word *tantra.* In that work, *tantra* is explained to mean "continuum." The *Guhyasamaja* further states that there are three types of continuums: (1) the continuum that is the basis, (2) the causal continuum, in which one applies various methods, and (3) the resultant continuum that is achieved using those methods. Con-sciousness therefore has three levels: one that is the basis, one in which we are tackling the mind so as to purify it, and the third level that is the result of dealing with mind, the state in which the mind has been completely purified. The first level corresponds to our present reality. I consider science to be the explanation of this ordinary reality. The second is an explanation of the techniques that we must apply, the method. This is Buddhist philosophy, involving Buddhist concepts. The third is the result.

These three understandings of the word *tantra* found in the Guhyasamaja—as basis, path, and result—are similar to the structure of the Buddha's first sermon on the four noble truths. When the Buddha first started to teach—when he taught or "turned" what we call the *first wheel of the doctrine*—he did so in three "repetitions," or, we might say, from three perspectives. In the first instance, he taught the actual *nature* of the four noble truths: the truths of suffering, its origin, its cessation, and the path leading to that cessation. In the second round, the Buddha explained the *function* of the four noble truths: what is to be abandoned and what is to be actualized—that suffering must be recognized, the origin of suffering must be eliminated, the cessation of suffering must be actualized, and the path must be cultivated. In the third round, or repetition, he explained the *result* that is obtained through that knowledge. We can see, therefore, that even in the first public sermon on the four noble truths, the Buddha presents, first, a theory of the nature of reality; second, the system of practice to be followed, the application of that knowledge; and third, the result achieved through the practice of the path.

I usually consider the Buddhist teachings to be of three types. The first is the Buddhist theory of reality, what I call "Buddhist science." The second, Buddhist philosophy, is based on the Buddhist theory of reality, on Buddhist science. Finally, there is Buddhist religion:

because it is possible for us to eliminate all negative emotions—to achieve such a result—it is worthwhile to engage in practice.

In Khöntön Peljor Lhündrub's text, we find a similar presentation. His work has three major sections. The first is an analysis of the fundamental ground of the mind, and how one goes about identifying the innate primordial state. That corresponds to understanding the nature of reality. In his second major subdivision, he explains how, having been introduced to that reality, one puts this understanding into practice. Then in the third section, he explains how the levels of realization and experience arise on the basis of that practice.

The Dialogue with Science

For more than twenty years now, we have had some serious discussions, or seminars, with scientists. These have taken the form of dialogues—what we might call "exercises in mutual learning." These conversations have focused on four fields: subatomic physics (such as quantum physics), cosmology, neurobiology, and psychology. The dialogue with quantum physics is really quite interesting, for there are many similarities between ideas held by Buddhists for over two thousand years and the latest findings of modern physicists.

Buddhist cosmology is basically the same as Western cosmology. However, in some Buddhist texts we find descriptions of the world that are obviously outdated: assertions, for example, that the world is flat, with a mountain called Meru at its center, and so forth. Because different Buddhist texts put forward different cosmological theories, Buddhists, in a sense, are at liberty to choose which of these theories they accept. In any case, as regards the physical universe, Buddhists can learn many things from modern science. It is really worthwhile for us to listen to what scientists have to say about cosmology and to study under them.

Next we come to neurobiology, the science that investigates the relationship between mental processes and the pattern of electrical activity in the neurons of the brain. Buddhists, particularly those who follow the Vajrayana, claim that mind and energy are related. Given this claim, it is quite interesting to investigate how the emotions function electrophysiologically at the neuronal level. As I have said, as far as the physical world is concerned, modern science is generally much more advanced. So it is very useful for us to learn from scientists. But the connection between neurons and consciousness is still not very clear. Here, some Buddhist explanations and experiences—some of the experiences of practitioners—may help us to gain a clearer picture about these relationships.

Some of my scientist friends provided us with the simple equipment to test the dying master I mentioned earlier. I think we waited for almost ten years for someone to die, in this particularly significant way, after the equipment became available. Before the machine was available, there had been quite a few occasions when such masters died, but there was no machine! Finally, last year, the two coincided. In any case, such projects where Buddhists and scientists engage in cooperative research ventures are both interesting and potentially fruitful avenues for investigating the functioning of the mind and its relation to bodily processes.

As regards the modern science of psychology, some refer to it as a "soft" science. This gives me the impression that psychology is still very young, that it is still in its infancy. The ancient Indian science of mind, by comparison, seems much more advanced. And, in fact, there is a lot of information in the Indian sciences of the mind that may be useful to modern scientists. In ancient Indian thought, for more than two or three thousand years, a distinction has been made between "sensory" and "mental" consciousness. In the course of our meetings with scientists, however, it became clear that contemporary psychology does not seem to clearly distinguish between the sensory level of experience and the mental level of experience. Such a distinction is very important. Sensory consciousness is intimately related to the body. As I mentioned earlier, gross mental consciousness is also related to the physical constituents of the body. But as the mental consciousness gets more and more subtle, there is more and more autonomy from the body. The states of mind that motivate behavior are not sensory in nature; here we are dealing with a strictly mental level of experience. In order to understand the function and operation of this mental level, which is really what determines a lot of our experiences of the world—our happiness and unhappiness, what is helpful and what is harmful— it is not sufficient simply to focus our observation and studies on the sensory level of experience.

In my meetings and discussions with scientists, my aim is always mutual understanding. I am not seeking from science some sort of backing for Buddhism. It is simply that on certain topics not much information is to be found in Buddhist science. In this case, it is helpful to learn from our scientific colleagues. On the other hand, Buddhist and ancient Indian thought is quite rich as far as the science of mind is concerned. In this case, it is natural that we share with scientists *our* understanding, some information that may give them a new perspective.

NALANDA: THE SOURCE
OF THE TIBETAN BUDDHIST TRADITION

Tibetan Buddhism is not the invention of Tibetans. Rather, it is quite clear that it derives from the pure lineage of the tradition of Nalanda Monastery in India, an institution founded at the beginning of the Common Era. The master Nagarjuna hailed from this institution, as did many other important philosophers and logicians. Although Tibetans became interested in Buddhism and began to study it as early as the seventh century, Buddhism did not really take hold in Tibet until a century later. A sound basis for Buddhism, the systematic establishment of Buddhist study and practice, therefore begins only in the eighth century. Two important Indian masters came to Tibet at this time at the invitation of the Tibetan emperor Trisong Detsen: Guru Padmasambhava and Shantarakshita.

Shantarakshita, who was very well known even in India, was mainly responsible for the exoteric teachings and giving monastic ordination. He was a great master, one of the great scholars of Nalanda Monastery. Shantarakshita was not only a scholar of Madhyamaka or Middle Way philosophy. His writings are still available to Tibetans in translation, and from these we can glean that he was a remarkable logician as well as a great Madhyamaka philosopher. So naturally, as one of the top scholars and one of the greatest practitioners of his day, a great monk of Nalanda, he can be considered the individual chiefly responsible for introducing the Buddhadharma to Tibet. Naturally, when the teacher is a philosopher or logician, he wants his students to follow this same trajectory. This makes sense; it is logical, is it not? Given that Buddhism was introduced into Tibet by one of the great scholars of Nalanda, it makes sense to say that the Tibetan tradition has basically followed the Nalanda tradition up to the present day. This is very clear.

When I myself began my scholarly studies of the tradition at a young age, I began by memorizing the root texts of that Nalanda tradition. In my own case, during this early period of my life, when I was a child of six or seven years of age, I had no real interest in Buddhism or in acquiring knowledge. I am sometimes considered the reincarnation of the Thirteenth Dalai Lama, but I wonder whether this is so. You see, when I was young, when I started learning these texts by heart, I had no real interest in them. I was a very reluctant student. My only interest was in playing. For this reason my tutor had to keep a whip by his side! In those days my elder brother and I—we were both monks—studied together. My tutor kept two whips. One whip was an ordinary whip, and one whip was a special, yellow whip. The yellow whip was considered a "holy" whip: the whip to be used on the holy person of the Dalai Lama. But as you can imagine, just because the whip was holy doesn't mean the pain was holy. I think the pain was the same! In any case, during those early years I continued my study of these texts, but out of fear.

All of us who have been trained in the classical, Tibetan tradition have studied these same texts, texts that we learned by heart. All of these root texts were written by the masters of Nalanda: Nagarjuna, Aryadeva, Arya Asanga, Vasubandhu, and so forth. Of course, alongside the root texts, we also study commentaries. There are many Indian and Tibetan commentaries, and we also read these works, but the fundamental texts all come from Nalanda. And even when the Tibetan commentaries wish to prove some important point, they always quote the texts of one or another of the well-known Indian masters. So the influence of the Nalanda tradition on Tibet is very clear.

The other major figure responsible for introducing Buddhism into Tibet was, of course, Padmasambhava. He was chiefly responsible for introducing the tantric methods, the Vajrayana. The Tibetan canon has a section called the Tengyur that consists of some two hundred volumes. These are the texts written by various Indian masters that were translated into Tibetan. Among these works, quite a number are tantric texts or commentaries written under the names of Nagarjuna, Aryadeva, and many other teachers associated with Nalanda. Therefore, the Tibetan Buddhist tradition—both the sutra and tantric traditions—comes from the lineage of Nalanda.

Tibetan Buddhism is a complete form of Buddhism. The Vinaya, or "Discipline," is the first of the three scriptural collections known as the *three baskets* (*Tripitaka*). The Tibetan texts belonging to the Vinaya are primarily based on texts like those found in the Pali canon. The two remaining baskets of the teachings are the Sutra Basket, the "Collection of Discourses," and the Abhidharma, or "Higher Knowledge." Texts belonging to these two baskets are also found in Pali, but those that were translated into Tibetan were primarily Sanskrit texts. In any case, the broader point is that the Tibetan canon contains teachings from all of the major strands of Indian Buddhism. This is what makes it a complete form of Buddhism.

Mind According to the Different Schools of Tibetan Buddhism

As I have said, a complete form of Buddhism was introduced and took hold in Tibet in the eighth century, during the so-called Early Translation Period. The Nyingma school of Tibetan Buddhism dates to this time. From the ninth through the eleventh centuries the Buddhadharma in Tibet went through a turbulent and difficult period. During this time, the Tibetan empire became decentralized, and Tibet became splintered into smaller kingdoms. After that, in the early part of the eleventh century, there begins the *Sarma*, or New Translation Period. This was the heyday of the translator Rinchen Zangpo and the time when the Indian master Atisha came to Tibet. It is during this second period of the dissemination of Buddhism that the other Tibetan traditions—for example, the Kadam, the Kagyü, and the Sakya schools—arose. The Gelug school was founded later. Each of these schools is itself a complete form of Buddhism. This means that each of these lineages contains the teachings of all the vehicles, including the Vajrayana, or tantric teachings.

To give an example of this completeness, consider the Nyingma school. The Nyingma tradition speaks of nine *yanas*, or "vehicles." These nine vehicles are grouped into three groups of three. The first three are the nontantric "vehicles that focus on the cause of suffering": (1) the vehicle of the disciples, or *shravakas*, (2) the vehicle of the self-enlightened ones, or *pratyekabuddhas*, and (3) the great vehicle, the Mahayana, also known as the vehicle of the bodhisattvas. The second set of three, known as the "vehicles that emphasize Vedic-like asceticism," are also known as the *outer tantras*. These are (4) the *kriya*, or "action," tantra, (5) the *upa* tantra, and (6) the *yoga* tantra. Then, finally, there are the three "vehicles that focus on the methods of powerful transformation," also known as the *inner tantras*: the (7) *maha*, or "great," (8) *anu*, "high," and (9) *ati*, "pinnacle." The *ati* is also known as Dzogchen, the "great perfection." We can see from this system of nine vehicles that a complete form of Buddhism is preserved in the Nyingma school.

Dzogchen chiefly focuses on the primordial innate mind known as *rigpa*, or "awareness," also sometimes referred to as Samantabhadra, the "All Good." Dzogchen contains unique methods that allow the adept to distinguish between what the tradition calls "ordinary mind," *sem*, and "primordial awareness," *rigpa*. In other contexts, even ordinary mind is said to be infused with a kind of awareness. But when distinguishing between *sem* and *rigpa*, *rigpa* refers to gnosis or wisdom. Ordinary mental states are more adventitious, more temporary; by nature, they fluctuate. *Rigpa* is devoid of such fluctuation; it is ever-present and unchanging, with neither beginning nor end. So Dzogchen draws a distinction between these two kinds of minds. The Dzogchen tradition is itself quite diverse. It has many different classes or levels of teaching—for example, the three cycles of Dzogchen teachings: the cycle of mind, the cycle of space, and the cycle of instructions.

Rigpa awareness, or Samantabhadra, is a primordially enlightened state, a quality of buddhahood that we all possess from beginningless time. However, this primordial quality of buddhahood is obscured by adventitious mental factors, our afflictions and other thought processes. Through practice, this primordial quality of buddhahood manifests. That is why, when all of the adventitious stains are cleansed, one is said to become *re*-awakened or *re*-enlightened. This is analogous to an idea found in the nontantric, Perfection of Wisdom teachings, where the nature of one's mind is referred to as *natural nirvana*—a state of natural, complete, and perfect nirvana that exists from beginningless time. This natural nirvana serves as the basis for the possibility of attaining the initial state of emancipation called *nirvana with residue*, and ultimately *nirvana without residue*, the final elimination of the afflictions and other obscurations in the state of enlightenment. If there were no natural nirvana, then actual nirvana would be impossible. Similarly, in Dzogchen teachings, the primordial buddhahood that we all possess is what allows for the possibility of achieving the re-awakened state, the re-attainment of buddhahood.

The nine vehicles of the Nyingma school are generally taught as a way of classifying the teachings of the Buddha. But there is a wonderful tradition where the nine vehicles are taught as different stages to be practiced by a single individual who is progressing along the spiritual path. In this more practice-oriented explanation of the nine vehicles, the meditation on the four noble truths constitutes the practice of the disciple's vehicle, the first of the nine vehicles. When the doctrine of the four noble truths is further elaborated— when the causal relationship between suffering and its origin and between cessation and the path are enlarged upon—this leads to the *twelve links of dependent origination*, both in their forward order (beginning with ignorance and ending with old age and death) and in reverse order. The twelve links constitute the main practice of the pratyekabuddhas, the self-enlightened ones; this is the second of the nine vehicles. Then the adept moves on to train in the generation of *bodhichitta*, the altruistic awakening mind, and to the practice of the six perfections, which includes *shamatha*, or calm abiding, and *vipashyana*, or insight. Here the practitioner is implementing the teachings of the bodhisattva vehicle, the causal vehicle of the perfections, which is the third vehicle. With this grounding, one then moves on to the next level, the practice of tantra, and specifically to *deity yoga*, where one visualizes either oneself in the form of a deity or a deity external to oneself who bestows blessings, powers, and so forth. Either way, it is through the practice of deity yoga that one progresses through the next three vehicles: *kriya*, *upa*, and *yoga*. Throughout these stages, one's practice of deity yoga becomes more and more clear. These so-called *generation-stage* practices are perfected in the *maha* yoga, at which point one moves on to the subtle energy practices of the *anu* yoga. At this point one has reached the stage of manipulating the energies within the channels of the body. When one reaches the great perfection, or *ati* yoga, one works to realize *rigpa* awareness. In this way, each stage serves as a prerequisite to the next, and together the nine vehicles comprise a holistic approach to practice in the spiritual life of a single individual.

Such an approach, where a vast body of literature is taken as individual instructions for practice, is also possible, for example, in regard to the Seven Treasuries of Longchenpa. I normally recommend that those who wish to practice Dzogchen proceed by first studying Longchenpa's *Treasury of Philosophical Tenets*, to follow that with study of his *Treasury of the Wish-Fulfilling Jewel*, and then to move to his *Mind at Ease*, part of his so-called Trilogy on Being at Ease. There is a custom of engaging in the study and practice of this latter text over a period of 145 days. From that point one proceeds to Longchenpa's *Treasury of the Supreme Vehicle* and then to his *Treasury of the Ultimate Expanse*. This represents a very systematic and holistic approach to the study of Dzogchen.

My more general point here is that it is very important to have an overall understanding of the basic framework of the Buddhist path. Of course, some fortunate individuals with positive karmic imprints from previous lives may be able to generate spiritual realization spontaneously by way of a tailored instruction from an experienced master. Such individuals are called "exceptional." But generally, for most practitioners, it is better to have this broad understanding of the structure of the whole Buddhist path and to engage in specific practices on the basis of that understanding.

Next we come to the Kagyü school. The Kagyü lineage mainly comes from the Indian master Naropa and his student Marpa, an eleventh-century Tibetan master. Marpa received teachings from many Indian masters; in particular, his main source for the Madhyamaka, or Middle Way, teachings is the Indian master Maitripa. It is quite clear that Maitripa follows the Madhyamaka view of Chandrakirti. One of the key teachings of the Kagyü tradition is Mahamudra, the "great seal." Mahamudra is of two types: a strictly sutra variety and a tantric variety. *Sutra Mahamudra* refers to the Madhyamaka view, to the meditation on emptiness, the lack of intrinsic existence. We find a reference to the Madhyamaka view as a "seal" even in the sutra teachings known as the *four seals* that characterize a view as being Buddhist: that all compounded things are impermanent, and so forth. The special or "uncommon" Mahamudra, however, is the tantric form, in which the subtle mind of clear light is generated using tantric techniques. One of the so-called six Dharmas of Naropa is a meditation on the clear light. The cultivation of this practice is what is called *tantric Mahamudra*. Here, it is principally the primordial innate mind mentioned above that brings about the essence of yogic insight, the essence of the path.

The Sakya tradition traces its lineage of instructions to the Indian master Virupa. The key instruction of the Sakya school is known as the Lamdré, the "path and its result." These Lamdré teachings, which are tantric teachings belonging to the highest yoga tantra class, are elaborated chiefly based on the *Hevajra Tantra*. The Lamdré instructions are taught using a framework known as the *three appearances* and the *three tantras*. The *three appearances* are (1) the appearances related to afflicted mental states, (2) the impure appearances, and (3) the pure appearances that belong to yogis. These three appearances correspond to the sutra teachings found in the first three vehicles of the Nyingma school: the vehicles of the disciples, self-enlightened ones, and bodhisattvas. The latter includes the teachings on the altruistic mind of enlightenment (*bodhichitta*). The Sakya Lamdré system does not contain specific teachings that correspond to the next three vehicles of the Nyingma school: the *kriya*, *upa*, and *yoga*. Instead, being a type of practice that belongs to the highest yoga tantra class, the next section of the Lamdré teachings corresponds to the *maha*, *anu*, and *ati* vehicles of the Nyingma school. This is a very important point: the *three tantras* of the Lamdré system correspond to the three meanings of the word *tantra* explained in the *Guhyasamaja Tantra* and mentioned earlier. In the Lamdré, they are called (1) the causal tantra, (2) the tantra as method, and (3) the tantra as result.

All of us already possess within us the *causal tantra*, or the "tantra that serves as the basis." This causal tantra is essentially what the Dzogchen texts refer to as *rigpa* awareness, or Samantabhadra. What the Sakya school calls the *awakening of the cause* is equivalent to what the Nyingma calls the identification of *rigpa* awareness. Although there are undoubtedly some differences in the way that the Sakya and Nyingma traditions explain the way this basic mind is to be identified, in the end, the ultimate intention of these two schools, the key point of these teachings, is the same. The causal tantra is what is to be identified, and it is to be identified on the basis of one's own experience. In the Sakya Lamdré system, the causal tantra is also referred to as *kunzhi*, the "basis, or foundation, of all things."

How does one come to a realization of this causal tantra? If memory serves me, one of the texts of Sakya Pandita, a great master of the Sakya tradition, provides an explanation of this point. Sakya Pandita states that as thoughts pass through the mind, between one thought and the next, the continuum of clear light, the basic mind, is uninterrupted. Generally speaking, there are two levels of thought: rough and subtle. The subtle type of thought found between one thought and the next is not identical to gnosis or wisdom. Nonetheless, identifying the basic mind, found in the interstices between thoughts, is important. It is also a practice found in both the Gelug and the Kagyü traditions of Mahamudra. In the Mahamudra teachings one identifies this basic mind by ceasing to dwell on the past and by stopping the train of thought that anticipates the future. In this way one halts all thoughts of past and future as soon as they begin to arise. Having done so, one remains in the present moment of consciousness, a state of mind that is fresh and uncontrived. When one achieves this, one has reached the subtle level of thought. This is precisely what is meant by *subtle thought*.

In Dzogchen, when one really identifies *rigpa* awareness, or Samantabhadra, one is said to have "apprehended the Dharma body." This is also called "distinguishing between the consciousness that is the basis of all and gnosis." Now when one has reached the subtle level of mind found between thoughts, one has not yet reached this state of pure *rigpa* awareness spoken of in Dzogchen—the kind of *rigpa* that distinguishes between the consciousness that is the basis of all and gnosis. Nonetheless, even in Dzogchen there is a practice analogous to remaining in the present moment. According to Dza Patrül Rinpoché's *Three Words that Hit the Mark*, by making an effort to repeatedly remain at the level of subtle thought, one achieves a special state of wonderment that is transparent and free of cogitation. This state, completely unaffected by thought, is a gentle resting in the present, uncontrived, self-arisen mind. According to Dzogchen, it is on the basis of *this* state that one truly identifies *rigpa*. The full identification of *rigpa* is then accomplished by receiving special blessings while one remains in such a state. In the nomenclature of the Sakya Lamdré system, the identification of the causal tantra, the basis of all, is a similarly subtle state of mind. Although this is not the actual primordial innate mind of clear light, the mind of clear light is intimately related to this state.

Various different types of *rigpa* are mentioned in the Dzogchen tradition: (1) *rigpa* as nature, (2) *rigpa* as the basis, and (3) the energy or effulgent expression of *rigpa*, called *rigpé tsel*. One also finds a distinction between "awareness itself," pure *rigpa*, and the "awareness that exists within consciousness," or *rigshé*. All ordinary, adventitious thoughts are said to be the "expressions of, or the effulgent manifestations of, awareness," *rigpé tsel*; and everything that is an "expression of awareness" is pervaded through and through by *rigshé*. When adventitious thoughts, like the afflicted emotions, manifest in our minds, since these are the expressions of *rigpa*, they are pervaded by *rigshé*. Because they are pervaded by, or infused with *rigshé*, even when the type of afflicted thought that possesses an object appears within the mind of the yogi, without following the object of that thought, without allowing the mind to be swayed by that object, the yogi, through the power of his or her experience, focuses on the ultimate, clear-light nature of the afflicted thought itself, and without having to abandon the affliction, rests within that state. This is by no means easy to achieve, but it is possible. In the terminology of the Sakya

Lamdré system, first one identifies the rough form of the causal tantra, the basis of all, which is the subtle level of thought. Then, based on that, one applies the yogic techniques of meditation, which roughly corresponds to the next of the Lamdré's stages, the *tantra as method*, or in the nomenclature of the Guhyasamaja system, the *tantra as path*. Finally, through the yogic practice of the path, one achieves the *tantra as result*, which is the Dharma body. Hence, parallels can be drawn between Dzogchen and the Sakya Lamdré system.

The tantra in general explains that one generates the meditational deity out of the realization of emptiness. This is true in all four classes of tantra: (1) action (*kriya*) tantra, (2) performance (*charya*) tantra, (3) yoga tantra, and (4) highest yoga tantra. But in highest yoga tantra, the mind that realizes emptiness is special. It is not a rough, ordinary mind. Instead, when one practices highest yoga tantra, one should possess a strong conviction that this mind, the mind out of which the deity is generated, is the primordial innate mind of clear light. To have such conviction, it is not enough to simply recite some words as part of a ritual. Rather, one must make the clear light appear within the mind, and—with a conviction that it is this primordial innate mind that is realizing emptiness—one achieves calm abiding and insight. Hence, the process of generating the deity out of emptiness is quite different in the lower tantras and in highest yoga tantra. In highest yoga tantra, one generates the deity out of the primordial innate mind of clear light.

When one reaches the *dzogrim* or *completion stage* of highest yoga tantra, one additionally resorts to practices involving the manipulation of the energy and drops within the channels of the subtle body. As a result of this practice, the grosser levels of mind wane or "dissolve." As the rougher, ordinary mind-energies become inactive, the subtler ones become active. The perspective of Dzogchen is somewhat different. In *that* system, because the ordinary, grosser levels of mind-energy are pervaded by *rigshé* even when ordinary thoughts are fully active, when these thoughts are made the object of the yogi's experience, it is possible to identify the quality of pure awareness in a natural way, without having to resort to completion-stage techniques. But according to the New Translation schools—the Sakya, Kagyü, and Gelug traditions—the subtle levels of mind-energy cannot be accessed while the ordinary, grosser ones are active. According to those schools, the clear-light mind only manifests *after* the rougher levels of consciousness have ceased. That is why the new schools emphasize the practice of the channels, energies, and drops.

The Sakya school speaks of the "union of clarity and emptiness." *Clarity* is the defining characteristic (Tib. *ngowo*) of the mind; *emptiness* is its nature (*rangzhin*). Their union, the union of clarity and emptiness, is ineffable, beyond words. Now the causal tantra, the basis of all, contains everything within it; it contains samsara, nirvana, and the spiritual paths. How, precisely, does it contain everything? How, for example, does it contain samsara? When we speak of samsara, we must remember that we are dealing with the mindstates of ordinary beings, beings who are still in training. In this context, the causal tantra, the basis of all, contains every phenomenon that exists in samsara "by virtue of the fact that it gives the world the characteristics that it has." And this is so because it is this causal tantra that causes the world to manifest, to appear the way it does. Next, the causal tantra is said to contain all of the realizations of the paths "by virtue of the good qualities it brings about." For example, the more one deepens one's faith, increases one's understanding of emptiness, or strengthens the practice of deity yoga, the more good qualities arise. These practices transform one. That is why the causal tantra is said to contain all the paths "by virtue of the good qualities it brings about." Finally, the causal tantra is said to contain all attainments "by virtue of the fact that it has the potential to create or generate those attainments." Because everything is contained within the causal tantra, the basis of all, samsara and nirvara are inseparable. This inseparability of samsara and nirvana is another fundamental tenet of the Sakya Lamdré system.

Perhaps this is as good a place as any to pause and take some questions.

Questions

Question: Is there some reason to prefer meditation on the nature of mind to meditation on anything else: for example, meditation on the nature of self or external phenomena?

His Holiness: The reason for emphasizing the mind is mainly to be found in tantra. As I mentioned earlier, everything ultimately depends on our motivation, and motivation is part of the mind. That is why, for example, the seventh-century Buddhist scholar Chandrakirti states:

> It has been taught that this very mind is what creates the
>   extreme diversity
> found in the universe of sentient beings and in their
>   environments.

All beings, without exception, arise from karma.

When mind has been abandoned, then karma ceases to exist.

All of the major concepts we have been discussing—the union of clarity and emptiness, the indivisibility of awareness and emptiness, the union of bliss and emptiness—involve an identical type of emptiness. This emptiness is no different from the emptiness of a pot or the emptiness of a sprout. Nonetheless, in tantra, the quality of the *agent* that is realizing the emptiness of mind—the clarity of this experience, and the way in which this mind is indivisible from its object, from emptiness—is quite different from what it is in the sutra teachings. In tantra, it is as if something's own essence were manifesting as its own realization. This can only take place when one takes the ultimate nature of mind as one's object, culminating in an indivisibility of awareness and emptiness. This is why the Indian master Aryadeva states that it is extremely important to realize the ultimate nature, or reality, of the mind, for it is the mind that is the root of samsara and nirvana. This is the way it is explained from a tantric perspective. From a sutra perspective, it is generally said that because there is a difference in the quality *of the object*, one begins by meditating on the lack of self, or emptiness, of the person, because it is easier to understand the emptiness of the person than it is to understand the emptiness of phenomena. However, from the perspective of highest yoga tantra, the realization of the ultimate nature of mind must come first.

When we do certain tantric rituals, we sometimes recite a mantra: *Om shunyata jñana vajra svabhava atmako ham.* In this mantra, the word *svabhava*, which means "essence," is referring to the fact that the reality being meditated upon is the very essence, or nature, of the agent doing the meditation. The *svabhava* in this first mantra is different from the *svabhava* in another important mantra: *Om svabhava shuddha sarva dharma svabhava shuddho ham.* In that latter mantra, no reference is being made to reality as the essence of the agent who is meditating.

Question: I'm wondering if Your Holiness thinks it is more difficult for Americans to focus their minds and to reach enlightenment? We are a culture that thrives on stimulation, excitement, pleasure, and doing everything very quickly. I think that meditation and centering oneself is extremely difficult in American society. Do you think it would be easier for Americans if we lived in a country with a slower pace, where people took more time to be present in their daily life?

His Holiness: Basically, I don't think there is a great deal of difference. It does not matter much whether one is Asian or Western. In fact, some of my American friends, who have spent many years in meditation, have obtained quite amazing results. These are Americans and not Tibetans! This shows that we are all basically the same. We all have the same human mind. It is true that external influences— one's surroundings and so forth—are important, but ultimately the nature of mind itself is *more* important. Each and every one of us has the same potential, the same mental quality. That is what I feel. However, if you, the questioner, are really serious about answering this question precisely, then you should do a thorough investigation. Interview people. Then perhaps you will get a clearer picture. From my side, I don't think there are that many differences.

Question: I try to practice mindfulness and being in the present moment, and I try to do this in a positive way. How does one do this when one's partner is doing exactly the opposite? How does one remain mindful and positive without being judgmental and without getting emotional?

His Holiness: That is why the texts recommend that practitioners maintain the companionship of people who share the same kind of outlook. But in your case, the important thing is that your partner be a warmhearted person. If your spouse has this attitude, then there should be no problem. Occasionally, get permission from your partner and spend some time in meditation. If you can't get permission, then you need to take into consideration your spouse's wishes and feelings. Take your partner as your teacher, your master, at least in your home. You should respect your spouse, provided that he or she is a good spouse, of course! One of the consolations of being a monk, a celibate person, is that we are truly independent. The married person, of course, is very happy for a short moment, but actually half of your freedom is lost! (Laughter.)

Question: How do you feel about the use of LSD and other psychedelic drugs to attain higher states of consciousness or spirituality?

His Holiness: Of course, I have to start by saying that I have no direct experience with psychedelics. But based on what I have heard from people who have had actual, firsthand experience, it seems that using such drugs tends to bring a greater profusion of illusions. Since we already have a lot of illusory experiences to begin with, why do we need additional illusory experiences? I think that those individuals engaged in serious practice should not rely on external substances, just simply try to cultivate the natural quality of mind. That is much better.

There is one final thing I want you to know: namely, that I am nothing special. I am just another human being, just like you. When you listen to me, you should think, "I am listening to another human being, *just* a human being." We all have the same potential. That is what makes one person's experience relevant to another. If you consider the Dalai Lama to be special, then my remarks become useless. If you have this idea that the Dalai Lama is extraordinary, you might say to yourself, "I can't possibly follow his advice. I can't benefit from his experience." That is just plain silly.

Some people even believe that the Dalai Lama has special healing powers. Since my surgery last year, I frequently tell people that if I really had healing powers, then my operation would not have been necessary. So my surgery is clear proof that I have no healing power! We are the same. This is very important. It is because we are the same that we can communicate, and it is because we are the same that you might derive some benefit from my words and experiences.

I will end here, with thanks to the organizers for this opportunity to address you, and with thanks to you, this very large audience present here today, for your willingness to listen. You really showed great attentiveness, for which I am very grateful. Finally, I wish to thank the University of California Santa Barbara. I greatly appreciate the fact that you have such a program for the study of Buddhism and Tibetan culture. Thank you all very much.

The Life of Khöntön Peljor Lhündrub

JOSÉ IGNACIO CABEZÓN

KHÖNTÖN PELJOR LHÜNDRUB[1] was born in 1561 into the famous Khön[2] clan, an ancient Tibetan family whose members include the founders and present-day throne holders of the Sakya school. Khöntönpa was born in the village of Kyong-gar[3] in the region of É.[4] His father, Tsewang Norgyé,[5] was an important figure in the transmission lineage of the *Magical Net Tantra*,[6] one of the most important tantric systems of the Nyingma school. Khöntön Rinpoché himself came to be considered one of the major figures in the transmission of this tantra.[7] Khöntönpa also played an important role in the history of the Gelug school. He was, for example, the fifteenth abbot of the Jé College of Sera,[8] and he came to be considered one of the lineage masters in the Gelug school's transmission of the "stages of the path" or *lamrim* teachings. Both the Nyingma and Gelug schools eventually came to consider him a reincarnation of the great Nyingma scholar-saint Dropugpa.[9] Khöntönpa therefore had close ties to the Sakya, Nyingma, and Gelug schools. As the work translated in these pages demonstrates, he also had a deep and profound knowledge of the teachings of the Kagyü school. It is not surprising, therefore, that Khöntönpa should be described in a variety of sources as a *rimé* master, a teacher who had an attitude of "impartiality with respect to both the Ancient and New schools."[10]

Khöntön Rinpoché's mother's, Gyelmo Dzom,[11] gave birth to three children, of which Khöntönpa was the eldest. Our sources describe him as an unusual child. For example, from the time he was an infant he could recite the seed syllable of the deity Manjushri. And instead of playing ordinary children's games, he would pretend to give teachings and empowerments to his peers. He learned to read and write simply from being shown the written letters. At the age of seven he developed a sense of renunciation—a strong sense of the transience of the pleasures of this life—by secretly reading his teacher's "mind training" or *lojong*[12] texts during breaks between classes.[13] His biographers also tell us that a sense of compassion for sentient beings never left him from the time when, as a child, he saw the suffering being experienced by a dog.

In 1570, at age ten, Khöntönpa's parents took him to receive teachings on refuge and the altruistic mind from the Third Dalai Lama, Sönam Gyatso.[14] Some sources state that he also took lay vows from the Third Dalai Lama at this time,[15] receiving the name Sönam Namgyel.[16] But the Fifth Dalai Lama[17] tells us that Khöntön Rinpoché received lay vows from the Third Dalai Lama around age seventeen, adding that his great predecessor picked the boy out of a large group of children brought before him and asked that the boy be "ordained."[18] This may be the last time that Khöntön Rinpoché would ever see the Third Dalai Lama, who left Tibet the following year (1578) to become the spiritual preceptor (*chönê*)[19] of the Mongolian ruler Altan Khan.[20] Gyelwa Sönam Gyatso would remain in Mongolia and in the Kokonor region of northeastern Tibet, preaching the doctrine and establishing monasteries, for most of the rest of his life.

In 1574, at age thirteen or fourteen, Khöntön Rinpoché's father took him for a visit to Dagpo College,[21] a Gelug monastery, where the boy received a number of long-life empowerments and some teachings, including Nyingma teachings, from the master of the college, Kelzang Gyatso.[22] He did not, however, enroll in the monastery at this time. Instead, the boy continued to live at home, where he was tutored by his father. Over the next several years Tsewang Norgyé imparted to his son various important Nyingma lineages, including the empowerment and teachings on the *Magical Net Tantra*, mentioned above. In his seventeenth year (1578) Khöntön Rinpoché met his other main Nyingma tutor, Nyida Sanggyé,[23] one of his father's own masters. Over the next two years Khöntön Peljor Lhündrub received from this famous master "introduction to the nature of mind," a variety of teachings on Dzogchen, as well as other instructions of both the scriptural and treasure (*terma*) genres.[24] In this way, Khöntön Rinpoché's teen years were spent mostly devoted to Nyingma tantric studies.

Not long after the death of his father, which occured when he was nineteen or twenty, Khöntön Rinpoché began to devote himself to Gelug scholastic studies. He officially entered Dagpo College in 1580, taking novice ordination at age twenty under the abbot of that institution, Lozang Gyatso.[25] Under this same teacher he also began his studies of the various subjects of the scholastic curriculum.[26] Khöntön Rinpoché began to write his own works during this time. For example, his *Teaching on the Middle Way View*[27] was written in his twenty-second year while he was still studying at Dagpo. The Fifth Dalai Lama tells us that this short text—whose authorship Khöntön Rinpoché initially concealed, perhaps out of humility— was remarkably well received. Shortly after completing his initial studies at Dagpo, Khöntönpa was appointed to an administrative position at his old home monastery of É Rigo Chöde.[28] He served in this capacity for a year and then went into retreat for a short time. When he returned to Dagpo, he began to teach.

Finishing his initial studies at Dagpo College, and already quite advanced in his knowledge of the classical Indian texts, Khöntönpa nonetheless decided to travel to Lhasa to enroll in the Jé College of Sera Monastery.[29] The Fifth Dalai Lama's biography of Khöntönpa sees this as confirmation of his past-life connections to Sera. In fact, the Great Fifth informs us that various events that occurred much later confirmed Khöntön Rinpoché to be the reincarnation not only of Jamchen Chöjé,[30] the founder of Sera Monastery, but also of Jetsün Chökyi Gyeltsen (or Jetsünpa),[31] the writer of the Sera Jé *yigchas*, or textbooks. At Sera, Khöntön Rinpoché deepened his knowledge of the Indian texts under the tutelage of Peljor Sönam Lhündrub[32] and Trinlé Lhündrub,[33] basing his studies on the textbooks of Jetsünpa. Not long after arriving at Sera, he did the traditional monastic "debate rounds" within the monastery and was awarded the *lingsé* degree.[34] This did not bring an end to his studies, however, for he continued to receive teachings from Trinlé Lhündrub on various texts not normally covered in the standard Gelug curriculum, texts like the four other works of Maitreya besides *Ornament of Realizations*. He also received various tantric initiations and teachings form his master during the breaks between the formal teaching periods. Shortly after completing the study of these additional texts, Khöntön Rinpoché sat for an additional set of examinations covering this broader corpus of literature at Tsetang Monastery,[35] obtaining the title of *rabjampa*,[36] "master of myriad treatises."

After completing his formal scholastic studies, Khöntönpa began to travel and take teachings from some of the more famous scholars in the region. For example, he went to Kyishö[37] to study the stages of the path literature under Ganden Chöjé Jampa Gyatso.[38] He also spent considerable time at Lhetag Monastery,[39] where he studied under Chennga Chöpel Zangpo.[40] From this renowned master he received instruction on Tsongkhapa's *Great Treatise on the Stages of the Path*[41] and on a wide range of topics of both sutra and tantra. His biographers tell us that he devoted himself to single-pointed contemplation on these texts until "he made realizations appear."

The Fifth Dalai Lama records an interesting episode in Khöntön Rinpoché's life that occured while while he was studying under Chenngapa. One day, Khöntön Rinpoché asked his teacher to engage in a prognostication to determine how long he (Khöntönpa) would live. The master told his young student that he should engage in the practice of Lhamo Shramana[42] so as to receive this information through his own dreams. The Fifth Dalai Lama records what transpired.

> A woman appeared to him [Khöntönpa] in his dream at dusk. She said, "You only have seven more years to live." Fearing that there were obstacles to accomplishing his many religious goals, he became worried and prayed again, asking her, "What will help to eliminate these interferences [to my lifespan]?" During a dream he had at dawn, she replied, "If you have eight statues of Amitabha and White Tara built, you will be able [to live to the age] of seventy-seven. But there is nothing you can do [to lengthen your lifespan] beyond that."[43]

Khöntön Rinpoché commissioned these statues on a yearly basis, and he lived to the precise age of seventy-seven.

Khöntönpa's other teachers during this somewhat peripatetic period of his life include the great Gomdé Namkha Gyeltsen,[44] from whom he received the empowerment and instructions on the generation and completion stages of the deity Yamantaka.[45] He also studied under Chöjé Rinchen Shenyen[46] at Pabongkha Hermitage.[47]

Khöntön Rinpoché received full ordination from Peljor Gyatso[48] (ordaining abbot) and Gendün Gyeltsen[49] ("secret preceptor") at Ganden Monastery[50] in 1594, when he was thirty-four years old. He was henceforth known under his new ordination name, Peljor Lhündrub. He then entered Gyümé,[51] the Tantric College of Lower Lhasa, where he studied for four years under the renowned Khedrub Namgyel Pelzang,[52] mastering all of the major tantric texts and rites of the Gelug tantric tradition. During breaks in his studies at the Tantric College he would often go to other monasteries, like Ganden and Drepung, for other tantric teachings and to engage in retreat. Despite several illnesses, Khöntönpa continued his practice with great perseverence, and his fame as a scholar and practitioner began to spread.[53] In 1599, he got word that his mother had taken seriously ill, and he decided to go home to see her. He learned that she had passed away while he was staying at Chonggyé,[54] on the road to É. He continued his journey home to perform his mother's funerary rituals.

On his return to Lhasa, Khöntön Rinpoché continued tantric studies at Sera under Peljor Sönam Lhündrub. He also turned his attention to poetics and prosody. During this period Khöntönpa accumulated a hundred thousand circumambulations of Lhasa's most famous temple, the Jokhang, and engaged in a variety of other merit-making practices on behalf of a patron, Nyangdren Rinchen Tselpa.[55] Throughout this entire time he continued to study both tantric and exoteric scholastic subjects under a variety of different masters.[56]

In 1601, at the age of forty, Khöntönpa was appointed chief teacher, or master (*lobpön*),[57] of the Nyima Tang College of Sangpu Monastery.[58] He held this position for five years. In 1603 the young Fourth Dalai Lama, Yönten Gyatso,[59] who had been born in Mongolia, was brought to Drepung, given novice vows, and installed in his seat, the Palace of Ganden. Four years into Khöntön Rinpoché's term at Nyima Tang, Trinlé Lhündrub, the abbot of the Sera Jé and Khöntön Rinpoché's teacher,[60] became gravely ill. Because of Khöntön Rinpoché's great learning, and because, in his teacher's words, "he was familiar with all of the difficult points of the philosophical tradition of Jé College,"[61] Trinlé Lhündrub instructed the monks of the college to appoint Khöntön Rinpoché as his successor. The monks followed their master's advice and installed Khöntön Rinpoché as the fifteenth abbot of Sera Jé in 1605.[62]

Even during his time as Jé abbot, Khöntönpa continued to receive instructions from the famous masters of the Gelug tradition. For example, in 1611 he went to Drepung to take teachings on the *Vajra Garland*[63] and other tantras under Penchen Lozang Chökyi Gyeltsen,[64] one of the greatest scholars of the day. Khöntön Rinpoché developed a close relationship with the Penchen Lama, who, it is said, praised him profusely, pronouncing him to be an extremely learned and holy being, and even prophesizing his later ascension to the position of Lord of Pabongkha.[65] During his years as master of the Jé College, Khöntön Rinpoché continued, whenever possible, to meet and to study under the greatest teachers of other schools

of Tibetan Buddhism: Jonang, Sakya, and Kagyü.[66] As the Fifth
Dalai Lama states, "Although he already possessed a great wealth
of erudition, his thirst for knowledge was never quenched."[67] So as
to make it clear that his teacher was not only a textual scholar but
also a great practitioner, the Great Fifth mentions many miraculous
events that took place during the rituals that Khöntön Rinpoché
presided over at the Jé College.[68]

Life as an abbot of Sera in the early seventeenth century was far
from easy. The Fifth Dalai Lama mentions some petty opposition
that Khöntön Rinpoché faced from his fellow monks during his
tenure as head of the Jé College, a reminder that the *densas*, the great
Gelug seats of learning, were not immune from internal squables.[69]
The greatest challenges that Khöntönpa faced, however, were not
from within the walls of the monastery but from the outside world
of Tibetan *realpolitik*. Over the previous decades the former rulers
of Tibet, the Rinpungpas,[70] had gradually lost power.[71] By the time
that Khöntön Rinpoché ascended to the abbacy of Sera Jé, the new
political force, the rulers of Tsang,[72] had substantial control of central and western Tibet.[73] Since the Tsangpa rulers were supporters
of the Karma Kagyü school, this meant that all of the monasteries
of Lhasa, including the great Gelug *densas*, were under the control
of the Tsangpa and Kagyü hierarchs. Sometimes the *densas* enjoyed a
great deal of freedom under the Tsangpas, but at other times those
freedoms were curtailed.

In 1616 the Fourth Dalai Lama, Yönten Gyatso, died. The following year, the Penchen Rinpoché became titular head of Sera and
Drepung.[74] The monks of these two Gelug institutions, resentful of
being under the control of the Tsang king, began to plan, in con-
junction with Khalkha Mongolian troops, an armed attack against

the Tsangpa forces stationed in Lhasa. Khöntön Rinpoché, the Fifth Dalai Lama tells us, tried his best to keep Sera monks from taking part in this uprising, and especially from resorting to violence, but his pleas were ignored. In their revolt of 1618, the Gelug monks and their Mongolian supporters proved no match for the Tsangpa troops under the leadership of Karma Tenkyong Wangpo.[75] Many monks were killed, and those that managed to avoid being massacred had to flee to Taglung, northeast of Lhasa.[76] The Penchen Rinpoché himself fled to Ngari[77] in northwestern Tibet, and Khöntön Rinpoché, fearing that he might have to become a refugee in Mongolia, went to Yerpa[78] to wait as events unfolded. Eventually, the Gelug monks were allowed to return from Taglung to their monasteries, and Khöntön Rinpoché himself returned from Yerpa, but Sera had been sacked and was in chaos. Khöntön Rinpoché tried his best to restore order to the institution, but the task was a mammoth one.[79] The situation must have been especially disheartening to Khöntönpa, given the fact that he had advocated a policy of nonconfrontation from the start.

It was probably as a result of these political problems,[80] both internal and external to Sera, that, after teaching at the monastery for about fourteen years, Khöntön Rinpoché stepped down as master of the Jé College. In 1619, at the age of fifty-eight, he moved from Sera to the nearby hermitage of Pabongkha,[81] where he devoted himself to more intensive practice.[82] In this ancient retreat, Khöntön Rinpoché devoted himself chiefly to meditation.[83] Khöntön Rinpoché made Pabongkha his base of operations for most of the rest of his life, staying mostly in his retreat throughout one of the most turbulent periods of Tibetan history.[84] Shortly after moving to Pabongkha, Khöntön Rinpoché began to teach Zurchen

Chöying Rangdröl,[85] who would later become one of the greatest masters of his day—a figure who, like his own teacher, was
acknowledged as a major lineage holder in both the Nyingma and
Gelug traditions.

In 1622 the young Fifth Dalai Lama was enthroned in the seat
of the Dalai Lamas, the so-called Palace of Ganden, located at
Drepung Monastery.[86] He took novice vows two years later.[87] In
1628 there was a lunar eclipse, and Khöntön Rinpoché interpreted
this as an omen of bad things to come. Although he did not travel
much while at Pabongkha, Khöntönpa did receive many visitors,
imparting empowerments and instructions to an entire generation
of young incarnate lamas and ordinary monks. In 1632 Khöntönpa
became very ill. When his disciples showed concern, he told them
that there was nothing to fear, reassuring them that he still had
about five years left to live. After recovering, he traveled the following year (1633) to the Palace of Ganden, the residence of the Fifth
Dalai Lama. There he gave his new student a variety of empowerments and instructions.[88] The Fifth Dalai Lama's regent, Desi
Sangyé Gyatso,[89] tells us that the Dalai Lama repeatedly told him
that Khöntön Rinpoché and the latter's student, Zurchen, "were his
two chief tutors during the early part of his life."[90]

In 1634 Khöntön Rinpoché once again became quite ill, and different rituals were done on his behalf at various institutions in and
around Lhasa, indicating the prestige that he had achieved by this
point. As on previous occasions, he recovered. In the following
year (1635), another year of great political upheaval in Tibet, the
Fifth Dalai Lama spent a fortnight at Pabongkha receiving empowerments, oral transmissions, and teachings from Khöntönpa on a
variety of topics from both the Nyingma and New traditions.

In a very personal portion of Khöntön Rinpoché's biography, the young Dalai Lama also tells us firsthand of the great reverence that Khöntön Rinpoché had for the teachings of Tsongkhapa, to the point that tears would well up in his eyes at the thought that the political turmoil of his day might lead to the decline of Tsongkhapa's tradition.[91] The Fifth Dalai Lama also adds that "because of his great knowledge of the nonsectarian tradition, even during his own lifetime there were many individuals who described his philosophical position as impure." "However," he continues, "the measure of having a really pure philosophical view is whether or not one respects this very master [Khöntön Rinpoché, an individual] who had authentic respect for the teachings of the victor Tsongkhapa."[92] Khöntönpa's great faith in Tsongkhapa is attested to in his own works. For example, in the final lines of his *History of the Yamantaka Lineage*, Khöntön Rinpoché refers to himself as "Peljor Lhündrub, a Khön monk, who, though born into the Manjushri Khön lineage of the glorious Sakyapas, came to understand and to have faith in the texts of the omniscient Lozang Drakpa [i.e., Tsongkhapa]."[93]

In addition to defending his teacher's doctrinal understanding, the Dalai Lama also recounts several anecdotes to confirm the depth of Khöntön Rinpoché's spiritual attainments. Despite the fact that his teacher always tried to hide his realization, the Dalai Lama states that he witnessed many instances that confirmed for him Khöntön Rinpoché's level of realization. For instance, he cites examples to show that Khöntön Rinpoché had great compassion for others, that he had perfected the generation stage of tantra, that his divinations were always accurate, and that he was capable of predicting the future. The Dalai Lama also expresses great admiration for his master's method of teaching: "In between the sessions of formal teachings, his conversations always consisted of historical anecdotes of the great events of the past, and his explanations were always flanked by the oral traditions of the lineage of the elders." "Never," he adds, "did I hear him say anything that was motivated by the three mental poisons [anger, desire, and ignorance], nor did he ever engage in stupid, idle chatter."[94] At the end of his two-week stay, as the young Dalai Lama was about to take leave of his teacher, Khöntön Rinpoché told his student that the time for him to take full ordination was at hand, and that he should invite the Penchen Rinpoché to serve as abbot during the ceremony.[95] This, in fact, happened a few years later in 1638.

In 1636 war once again broke out in Lhasa, and the Fifth Dalai Lama and his entourage took refuge at the Gyel Lhakhang Monastery in Penyül.[96] Once the threat had subsided, the Dalai Lama returned to the capital, stopping at Pabongkha on the way back to his residence at Drepung. Although the Dalai Lama had planned to spend a few months receiving teachings from Khöntön Rinpoché at the hermitage, circumstances did not allow him to remain for more than ten days. Nonetheless, Khöntönpa managed to give his student many special instructions during this time. He also warned him of his own (i.e., of Khöntönpa's) impending death: "I am now seventy-six years old, and I don't know how much longer I will live."[97] The young Dalai Lama asked his teacher where he would be reborn. The master replied that if he had any choice in the matter, he would not be reborn in China, Mongolia, or central or western Tibet. Lest the reader assume from this response that Khöntön Rinpoché had seen too much strife on the Tibetan plateau and was ready to leave the Tibetan world behind him, the Dalai Lama assures us that his teacher's words should not be taken literally.[98]

This is, of course, significant, since eventually the Changkya lamas would come to be recognized as the reincarnations of Khöntön Peljor Lhündrub.

In the seventh Tibetan month of 1636, the victorious Khalkha Mongolian general Arslang arrived in Lhasa. Arslang visited Khöntön Rinpoché as part of his tour of the city. Various bad weather omens, including hail, occured during Arslang's visit to Pabongkha, and rituals had to be done on Arslang's behalf. Arslang asked Khöntön Rinpoché whether a reconciliation between him and his estranged father were possible. The master replied that it was not, that serious obstacles still remained.[99] And, in fact, it would not be long before Arslang's father, Tsogtu Taiji, would order the murder of his own son for having betrayed him.

By 1637 life at Pabongkha returned to normal. The monks' rainy season retreat was observed, and the traditional ritual cycles were performed. But then various bad omens began to appear. On the eighth day of the eighth Tibetan month, at the conclusion of the rainy season retreat, Khöntön Rinpoché became slightly ill. His condition worsened, but he maintained a joyful attitude, even smiling and greeting visitors who came to see him. On the ninth and tenth he took to looking repeatedly into space and laughing, his expression one of utter joy. The Dalai Lama tells us that what was transpiring, "although of great significance, is beyond anyone's ability to put into words."[100] Khöntön Rinpoché, he then recounts, "actualized the profound, peaceful, unelaborated state of the clear-light Dharma body on the evening of the eleventh." The Fifth Dalai Lama, who was twenty-one years old at the time, was traveling, and so, in his words, "missed the opportunity to see [Khöntön Rinpoché] make his passage to the pure land." Two days later, however, he did have the chance to see his teacher's body in the type of meditative equipoise described by His Holiness earlier in this book, a state known as *tugdam*. Various miraculous signs appeared. Khöntön Rinpoché's body emitted a pleasant fragrance and a glow that would not dissipate. A canopy of rainbow light took shape in a clear sky, a sign that often accompanies the passing of a Dzogchen master. On the nineteenth, eight days after he stopped breathing, the two "drops," one white and one red, appeared from the great master's nostrils, indicating that Khöntön Rinpoché had passed from "the clear light of death of the Dharma body into the enjoyment body of the intermediate state."[101] The funeral services were then performed.[102] As foretold in his dream by the goddess Shramana decades earlier, Khöntön Rinpoché died at the age of seventy-seven.[103]

With offerings made by the Mongolian ruler Gushri Khan[104] and others, the Fifth Dalai Lama built a silver funerary stupa at Pabong-kha to house his teacher's remains, and he commissioned a life-size statue of Khöntönpa for the hermitage.[105] Various magical signs occurred on the day the body was finally placed inside the stupa reliquary. As a tribute to his teacher, the Dalai Lama also expanded the Pabongkha retreat center and generously endowed it with fields, pastures, and livestock.[106] Khöntön Rinpoché was an important influence on the Great Fifth, both intellectually and spiritually. His most extensive biography is the one written by the Dalai Lama, his most famous student.[107]

Introduction to Khöntön Peljor Lhündrub's
Wish-Fulfilling Jewel of the Oral Tradition

José Ignacio Cabezón

Introduction

Tibetan Buddhists refer to the theory of reality—the final nature of phenomena, the way things are—as *tawa*.[108] The word *tawa* is often translated "view" or "theory," but these terms do not completely capture the Tibetan meaning, nor that of its Sanskrit equivalent, *darshana*. "Viewing" is a passive activity, implying little if any rational or conceptual activity on the part of the viewer. "Theorizing," while capturing this more active, rational dimension of the word *tawa*, is, at least in common English parlance, a strictly intellectual pursuit. But in the Tibetan tradition *tawa* is more than mere philosophy. It is something to be internalized, the raw material for spiritual practice that culminates in human transformation. His Holiness alludes to this in the first part of this book when he speaks of the distinction between Buddhist science on the one hand, and the application of that science in the context of Buddhist practice on the other. Meditation, or *gom*,[109] is the main bridge between the intellect (science) and the transformative experience that is the goal of human existence (buddhahood, the "result"). When internalized through meditation, the "view" becomes insight or wisdom. This wisdom is the chief antidote to suffering.

Throughout its 2,500-year history, the greatest minds of Buddhist India and Tibet have offered interpretations of the view. Even in the scriptural canon, in the writings attributed to the Buddha himself, different theories of reality can be found. How does the tradition explain this diversity of perspectives on the nature of reality? The Tibetan scholar Zhabdrung Mingyur Dorjé (b. 1675) put it this way:

> Because the Buddha was compassionate and skillful in his methods, he taught various different entryways into the doctrine. But this does not mean that these [doctrines] are *truly* distinct. It was for the sake of training disciples with various proclivities, intellectual abilities, and needs that he taught according to their individual minds.[110]

Despite attempts (like Mingyur Dorjé's) to reconcile the differences in the Buddha's teachings, the different interpretations of reality found in the scriptures gave rise to different philosophical and contemplative traditions. Buddhist thinkers of later generations attempted to bring order to these different perspectives in a variety of ways. Both in India and Tibet, different schemes[111] were elaborated to classify the different interpretations of reality, to distinguish[112] one interpretation from another, and to suggest which interpretation was "definitive." Differences of opinion concerning the view sometimes led to polemics[113]—debates in which scholars attempted to prove the superiority of one interpretation over another. None of this should be very surprising. Like all great intellectual and spiritual traditions, Buddhism is not homogeneous, and Buddhist philosophers have not always seen eye to eye on every point of doctrine or practice. As Mingyur Dorjé states, people have different "proclivities, intellectual abilities, and needs."

So differences of opinion concerning the correct interpretation of reality have undoubtedly existed. But if there have been attempts to distinguish between different perspectives on the view, there have also been attempts to *unify* them: to point to commonalities rather than to differences, to emphasize the intersections rather than the disjunctions between different theories. Khöntön Peljor Lhündrub's *Wish-Fulfilling Jewel* belongs to this more ecumenical approach.

Centuries before Khöntönpa, three great traditions of the view, or *tawa*, had already been identified by a variety of Tibetan thinkers:

- The Madhyamaka, or "Middle Way"—sometimes called Uma Chenpo,[114] the "Great Middle Way"—which has its roots in the writings of the Indian sage Nagarjuna (ca. second century C.E.)
- Mahamudra, the "Great Seal"—or, in Tibetan, Chagya Chenpo—which has its source in the tantras of the *Sarma* or New schools and in the writings (and especially the "songs") of the great Indian tantric saints (*mahasiddhas*)
- The Great Perfection, or Dzogchen, with its chief source in the tantras and revealed treasures, the *terma*, of the Nyingma school of Tibetan Buddhism

Although the view was the focal point of various other practice systems,[115] for centuries, these three—the Middle Way, Mahamudra, and Dzogchen—occupied a special place. Mention of this triad is found centuries before Khöntön Rinpoché. For example, half a millenium earlier the great Tibetan yogi Milarepa (1052–1135) would "sing":

> The Great Perfection takes no sides.
> If it takes sides, it is not the Great Perfection.
> The Great Seal doesn't negate or affirm.
> If there is negation or affirmation, it is not the Great Seal…
> In the Great Middle Way, there is no identity at which to
>   grasp.
> If identity is grasped at, then it is not the Great Middle Way.[116]

At about the same time that Jetsün Milarepa was comparing these three approaches to the view, the famous woman saint Machig Labdrön (b. 1055) was claiming that her famous system of meditation called Cutting or Severance (Chö)[117] was nothing other than the Great Middle Way, the Great Seal, and the Great Perfection.[118] Two centuries after that, the Third Karmapa, Rangjung Dorjé (1284–1339), states:

> This freedom from cogitation is the Great Seal.
> The freedom from extremes is the Great Middle Way.
> Encompassing everything, it is also called the Great
>   Perfection.
> May I obtain confidence in this single reality that, once
>   understood, brings about all realizations.[119]

A few decades later, the great Nyingma scholar-saint Longchen Rabjampa (1308–64) would write:

It is the perfection of wisdom, the Middle Way.
It is what pacifies proliferations and suffering, the Great Seal.
It is the essential reality, the Great Perfection.
The primordially extinguished state, the basic reality,
is the clear light, the mind's nature, the self-arisen gnosis.
Although it is labeled using many names, the meaning [of
these systems] is one in nature.[120]

Like his famous predecessors, Khöntön Rinpoché was interested in the similarities that exist between these three great traditions of the view. While the *Wish-Fulfilling Jewel* is chiefly a practical guide to meditation on the nature of mind, Khöntönpa also has other agendas: to demonstrate (1) that the Madhyamaka, Mahamudra, and Dzogchen are not contradictory as theories of reality, and (2) that they could be integrated into a coherent system of meditation.

Khöntönpa was not the only Tibetan scholar of his generation to point to the commonalities between the different approaches to the view.[121] His younger contemporary (and teacher), the First Penchen Lama, wrote a work called *Mahamudra According to the Tradition of the Precious Oral Lineage of the Geden* (i.e., *Gelug*).[122] Although Penchen Rinpoché's work focuses chiefly on Mahamudra, it has many resonances with Khöntönpa's little book, stressing the similarities between different systems of practice. In some verses found at the beginning of the work, the Penchen Lama states:

There are many distinct ways of naming [the traditions of meditation on the view]:
There are [five traditions of Mahamudra]: Coemergence, the Amulet Box,

the Five-Part [Instruction], Equal Taste, and the Four
  Letters.
[There are also systems like] the Pacifier, Severence, the
  Great Perfection,
teaching manuals on the view, and so forth.
When these [various traditions] are analyzed by yogis
who are experts in the scriptures and logic of the highest
  meaning
and who really possess spiritual experience,
the intention [of all of these different traditions] will be seen
  to boil down to the same thing.[123]

Like the Penchen Lama and Khöntönpa, many other scholars in
the history of Tibetan Buddhism have emphasized a more ecumenical, trans-sectarian approach to the view.[124] But few works in
the history of Tibetan literature attempt as broad and detailed a
reconciliation of *all three* major traditions of the view—Madhyamaka, Mahamudra, and Dzogchen—as Khöntön Rinpoché's *Wish-
Fulfilling Jewel.* Certainly no parallel work exists, to my knowledge,
in the Gelug school.

  The various passages cited above may appear to imply an exact
equivalence between Madhyamaka, Mahamudra, and Dzogchen:
that these three systems are simply alternative paths to the same
goal. But the relationship between these three approaches to the
view is a bit more complex than implied by the claim of simple
equivalence. What then *is* this relationship between the Madhyamaka, Mahamudra, and the Great Perfection? The structural relationship between the three is not one of simple identity. During
his visit to Santa Barbara, His Holiness made a remark to me that

caused me to give some thought to this question. "One should not think," His Holiness said, "that there is such a thing as the practice of Mahamudra or Dzogchen apart from a thorough grounding in Madhyamaka." As he put it, the realization of Mahamudra or of Dzogchen *rigpa* is impossible apart from an understanding of emptiness as taught in the Madhyamaka texts of Nagarjuna and Chandrakirti—as impossible as a "white crow." In other words, Madhyamaka forms the basis for *all* the great practice traditions of the view, serving as the ground for Mahamudra and Dzogchen. That Madhyamaka serves as the underpinning for these other systems of meditation on the nature of reality is a position that has been espoused by a number of Tibetan scholars up to the present. For example, the great Nyingma scholar-yogi Do Ngag Chökyi Gyatso (1903–57) states:

> Mahamudra and Dzogchen ought to be chiefly considered the ultimate, great vajra-yogas of the indivisible realization of method and wisdom found in the highest tantric systems, the highest yogas of the new and old tantras, respectively. The Madhyamaka is the pinnacle of all the philosophical schools from the viewpoint of wisdom; it is the superior view (*tawa*) that, following the sutras of definitive meaning, leads to the realization of the profound realilty advocated by those who espouse the view [that everything] lacks intrinsic nature. That the [Madhaymaka] is the *sole* view of all of the sutras and tantras is accepted, almost without exception, by countless numbers of scholar-adepts, chief among them Rongzom Pandita, the great, omniscient Longchen

Rabjampa, the great Sakya Penchen, a follower of the New [Translation] tradition, and Lord Tsongkhapa and his spiritual heirs.[125]

Do Ngag Chökyi Gyatso is here making several important points. There is a difference between Mahamudra and Dzogchen, on the one hand, and Madhyamaka, on the other. Mahamudra and Dzogchen are the names given to the highest realizations of the most advanced tantric meditation practices of the New and Old Translation schools, respectively. As His Holiness states earlier in this book, these special tantric techniques all have as their goal the manifestation of the subtlemost mind within the mental continuum of the adept. The methods of tantra are unique in their ability to make manifest this subtle mind. Without relying on the techniques elaborated in tantra, no access to the primordial, innate mind of clear light is possible. But if the methods of the tantras are unique and essential to the project of enlightenment, so too is the "view" that undergirds the tantras. The philosophical underpinning of all of these tantric systems—Mahamudra, Dzogchen, and the Sakya-pas' Lamdré—is the Madhyamaka. From the side of wisdom, as Do Ngag Chökyi Gyatso states, there is no view higher than the Madhyamaka theory of emptiness. The Madhyamaka is therefore the fundamental view of both sutra and tantra. This, he adds, is the position of the greatest scholars of Tibet. It is also the position of Khöntön Peljor Lhündrub, the author of *The Wish-Fulfilling Jewel.*

Khöntönpa's text is sufficiently clear that a rehearsal of its contents is unnecessary. As His Holiness states, the work is structured around the well-known tripartite division of "basis, path, and result." More practically than theoretically oriented, the work leads the reader on a journey from the very beginning of Buddhist practice to the realization of the most sublime goal of buddhahood. The focus throughout is on the realizion of the nature of mind, and Khöntönpa lucidly explains the steps that must be followed in order to come to such a realization, to stabilize and enhance it, and to use this as the means of transforming one's mind for the benefit of others.

Khöntön Rinpoché authored over thirty works covering a wide range of genres and topics (see appendix 1), but aside from the text translated in these pages, only four of his other works still survive:

1. A subcommentary to Gyeltsab Jé's[126] commentary to the *Ornament of Realizations*[127]
2. A commentary on a prayer for rebirth in the heaven of Sukhavati[128]
3. The biographies of the masters of the lineage of the deity Yamantaka[129]
4. And a text called *Profound Instructions on Going for Refuge to the Three Jewels: An Oral Tradition with Three Special Features*[130]

The text translated here, *The Wish-Fulfilling Jewel of the Oral Tradition*, written in 1609,[131] was believed to have been lost until a copy was recently found and published in eastern Tibet. For those who read Tibetan, a newly edited version of the text is available free for download from the Wisdom Publications website (wisdompubs.org) at the page for the present volume. The work gives us a glimpse of Khöntönpa's synthetic style and a taste of his nonsectarian approach to the view. Quoting liberally from various Indian sources, and from some of the most famous masters of the Nyingma, Kagyü, Sakya, and Gelug traditions, the text is also witness to Khöntön Rinpoché's incredible command of Buddhist literature, both Indian and Tibetan.

It is a great pleasure to be able to present this annotated translation of Khöntön Rinpoché's work alongside His Holiness's reflections on the nature of mind, for it is precisely meditation on the nature of mind, as the reader will see, that Khöntönpa considers the bridge between these three great approaches to the Buddhist "view" of reality. As the Lord Milarepa states:

> To ascertain the view, look at your own mind.
> Those who search for the view apart from the mind
> are like rich people searching for wealth.[132]

It would be foolish for those who are wealthy to search for money apart from what already exists under their very noses in their own coffers. Likewise, the view is closer to us "than our own jugular veins," as the Tibetan saying goes. All we have to do is to turn our attention to the nature of our own minds.

The Wish-Fulfilling Jewel of the Oral Tradition:
Instructions on Identifying the Shared View of Reality[133]

KHÖNTÖN PELJOR LHÜNDRUB
TRANSLATED BY JOSÉ IGNACIO CABEZÓN

Homage to the master, the deva daki.

Homage to you, glorious master, whose nature is the three objects
    of refuge,
who has perfectly united the pieces of the orbs of the sun of
    knowledge and the moon of empathy.
Endowed with a net of white rays of light, your majestic
    actions,
you are encircled by millions of stars and constellations, the
    awareness holders.

I bow down to the hosts of tutelary deities,
who play out the great bliss with their illusory dance:
the primordial lord Samantabhadra, Heruka,
the lord Vajradhara, the buddhas of the five families, and the
    hosts of peaceful and wrathful ones.

I bow down to Vajradharma,[134] essence of all the secrets of the
    conquerors,
Prahevajra, Manjushrimitra,
Shrisimha, the awareness holder Padmasambhava,

Vairo[tsana], and the others [who together make up] the lineage
   of the early translations;
and to Sarahapa, Nagarjunapada, and his son Aryadeva,
Naropa, Maitripa, Lord Atisha, and his spiritual heir Dromtönpa,
Dampa Sangyé, Marpa, and his spiritual heir Milarepa.

Having paid homage to Manjughosha Lama [i.e., Tsongkhapa],
who revealed the great innate bliss as clearly as a treasure in the
   palm of one's hand,
and to Gampo[135] and his spiritual sons,
I will now write down their oral instructions.

IT IS GENERALLY believed that in the Land of Snows the great
scholar-practitioners of the past accept three Mahayana formula-
tions of the view of reality: (1) the Great Middle Way, (2) the
Great Seal, and (3) the Great Perfection. What is more, there are
many ways of interpreting these three. From among these various
interpretations, there is one tradition, accepted by Gampo and his
spiritual heirs, that is based on the essential instructions of the
great awareness holder Padmasambhava. This interpretation—
called the "view of the Dharma in general" or the "identification
of the general and pervasive view"—is a way of teaching the view
of reality as a unified whole, a method of instruction that stresses
the commonalities between these three methods of interpretation
and that harmonizes the points related to their practice. [382] Since
this approach is what is taught prior to the transmissions of the
uncommon instructions of the seminal essence (*nyingtig*),[136] this is
the subject matter of my explanation.

I. How, according to the beliefs of the masters of yore, one goes about identifying the general and pervasive view of reality
A. The introductory material
1. The general introduction
a. A history of this doctrine and this lineage, taught for the sake of generating trust in the instructions

This part of the instructions includes, on the one hand, an explanation of the greatness of the lineage and the biographies of the lineage masters and, on the other, an explanation of the greatness of the doctrine being taught. This will not be explained here. Instead, you should understand it by consulting other sources.[137]

b. How to train the mind in the common path, taught for the sake of making one a fit vessel for the profound path

This includes explanations of:

- Relying on the master, the root of all spiritual accomplishments
- Contemplating how this life, filled with leisure and opportunity, is difficult to find and is therefore extremely meaningful
- Contemplating how this human life is easily destroyed and how the time of death is uncertain
- Contemplating the suffering of the lower realms and how to go for refuge
- Adopting certain behaviors and turning away from others based on the contemplation of the results of good and bad karma
- Contemplating the faults of samsara and accomplishing the state of mind that overturns attachment [to higher rebirths]
- Having contemplated the way in which all sentient beings

have acted as one's mothers and fathers, training in love, compassion, and the altruistic mind of enlightenment (*bodhichitta*)

▸ Having contemplated the qualities of a buddha, training in the practices of bodhisattvas so as to attain that state [of enlightenment for the sake of others]

These meditations should be known in greater detail from the stages of the path (*lamrim*) literature.[138]

2. The special/uncommon introductory practices
This includes:

▸ Chiefly, obtaining a pure empowerment[139]
▸ Maintaining the commitments and vows [taken during an empowerment or through ordination][140]
▸ As a preliminary to each session of meditation, performing the rituals of going for refuge, generating the awakening mind, and reciting the hundred-syllable mantra of the deity Vajrasattva[141]
▸ Accumulating *kusulu* offerings[142]
▸ The yoga of the spiritual master[143]

These should all be understood from other sources.

B. The actual explanation
1. How to analyze the fundamental ground of the mind and how to identify the innate primordial state
a. Searching for the hidden dimension[144] of reality by analyzing how the mind arises, abides, and moves on

Make sure that your practice of the preliminaries is not just from the mouth—in other words, that it is not mere words—but that it transforms your mental continuum [383] to the point that certainty actually arises.[145] Melding the lama's mind into union with your own through the practice of the yoga of the spiritual master, relax and then settle into a state of primordial devotion. Find the still point of the mind—that is, accustom yourself to this for a short time.

Once you have done this, ask yourself: "Who is the agent responsible for the fact that the buddhas of all three times have been liberated from all the faults of existence and peace,[146] and who is the agent responsible for the fact that all of us sentient beings wander in the six realms and experience various kinds of suffering? Is the responsible party the god Brahma? Is it Vishnu? Is it Ishvara? Is a permanent soul responsible? Of my body, speech, and mind, which is responsible [for the fact that buddhas do not suffer but we do]? Where do the phenomena that belong to the categories of samsara and nirvana come from? What brings them into existence?"

The root of every phenomenon—whether the phenomenon belongs to the category of appearances/existence, samsara, nirvana, or the paths—*is your very own mind.* As Saraha puts it:

> Every phenomenon is your own mind.
> Apart from the mind there is no other phenomenon, not
>   even the slightest.[147]

And also:

> The mind alone is the seed of everything;
> existence and nirvana are projected out of mind.

I bow down to the mind that, like a wish-fulfilling jewel, brings me to my desired goal.[148]

Moreover, the *Scripture of the Ten Stages* states:

Hey you, children of the Conqueror! These three worlds[149] are only mind![150]

Now analyze the foundation of that mind that is the source of everything by asking whence it arose, where it abides, and where it goes. First, what is its source? Is its source the outer, inanimate world? Does that mind arise from earth and stones? From mountains and caves? From plants, trees, and forests? And *how* does it arise—that is, in what way does it arise? Does it arise from an animate cause in the world of sentient beings? Does it arise from the outer or inner parts of your own body or from those of your parents or relatives? Do a thorough analysis and examination, relying on questions such as these, and meditate on this.

Next, do a detailed analysis and examination of this thing called "my own mind": "You, thinker of wild thoughts, flying out to cognize everything you can, from where do you originally come? What is your nature? What function do you perform? Where in regard to the body—inside or outside, above or below—are you residing right now? And *how* do you abide? In the end, where do you go? If you are an empty thing that comes from nowhere and goes nowhere, how can you be the cause of error and of my wandering in the six realms?" Do such a detailed analysis.

If your interrogation is not very clear, you should resort to special instructions [to counteract the problem], like the one given by the Lord Atisha, who taught that:

When an afflicted misconception arises,

pursue it like a falcon pursues a sparrow:

start circling it as your object, and isolating it, swoop in.

Once you have it in your talons, crush it![151]

An individual in whom the negative emotion of desire predominates searches for the mind using a beautiful object. [384] Meditate again and again on that beautiful thing, visualizing what you desire in front of you. When it is so clear that it is as if you were actually looking at it, and attachment for the object has arisen in you, then look to see whether the way in which the beautiful object appears to that desire is the way in which it actually exists. Look to see what the desire itself is like: what shape and color the desire has, what its nature and function are. Look to see where that desiring mind comes from in the first place and where it is right now. Is it abiding inside or outside the body?

The type of person for whom anger is the predominant emotion should search for the mind using an enemy as his or her object. Visualize before you the enemy who causes you troubles, and think again and again of all the harmful things he or she has done to you. When a strong burst of anger arises in you, and while the whole of your mind is consumed by that anger, focus on the anger using a very small portion of your mind and see how the enemy appears to it. When your enemy appears to you in such a way that you think, "he or she exists from his or her own side without depending on anything else; he or she is a concrete reality," then you have identified how the object of negation[152] appears to the mind. Then analyze the object of your anger as follows: "If that enemy existed without relying on anything else, then how could it be that, at the beginning of his or her life, this enemy has a father and mother as a cause and condition for his or her birth? How could it be that, in the middle, he or she is subject to concordant and discordant conditions?[153] How could it be that at present, when I bring him/her to mind, anger arises, but that when I do *not* bring this enemy to mind and instead forget him/her, anger does not arise? And how is it that at the end of his/her life, at the time of death and so on, he or she must cease?" Also, look at the anger itself and ask yourself, "What is its shape? What is its color, its nature, and its function?"

A person attached to other people looks for the mind with respect to his or her relations. First you visualize your close relations in front of you. Recollect and make clear to yourself all of the ways in which they have benefited you. Then look to see whether or not that object exists as it is appearing to you.

Likewise, a merchant searches for the mind with respect to the amount of profit he or she might make. A person who is hungry and thirsty searches for the mind with respect to food and drink. A proud person searches for the mind with respect to the source of his or her pride, and so forth. You should know which object to prescribe based on the personality of the student.

The same method applies to various types of spiritual people. The faithful should search for the mind with respect to the spiritual master. Over and over again recollect, and make vividly present in your mind, the body of the master in whom you have faith; recollect the timbre of his or her speech and the knowledge of his or her mind. Then ask yourself whether the master appears to your faith-filled mind as he or she actually exists; ask yourself whether that faith exists inside or outside of your body, and what its nature and function are.

Intellectuals should search for the mind with respect to the cultural sciences. [385] Those who like to argue should search for the mind with respect to philosophical speculation. Shravakas[154] should search for the mind with respect to the rules of monastic discipline. Bodhisattvas should search for the mind with respect to compassion. Those who are practicing the generation stage of tantra[155] should search for the mind with respect to the deity's body. Those who are practicing the stage of completion should search for the mind with respect to the channels and wind energies.[156] The method of interrogation is in each case as above.

When, from time to time, the clarity of those mental states increases, stop conceptualizing and focusing on the nature of the object and of the mind itself. And ceasing other forms of thinking, naturally settle into the natural state. Search for the nature of mind alternating between [active conceptual questioning and nonconceptual settling of the mind into the natural state]. It is necessary to repeatedly use this method of refined analysis of the mind even after you have identified the mind's nature. As Urgyen Rinpoché [i.e., Padmasambhava] has said,

> Engage steadfastly in cycles of emptiness meditation wherein
>   conceptual thought is driven back into its
>   liberated state
> through calmly abiding on the original ground that
>   is emptiness.[157]

And also:

> When gross conceptualization occurs, search for the agent
>   of thought internally.

It is not necessary to intentionally abandon or accept
    anything; just place your mind in its natural state.

And Dampa Rinpoché[158] has said,

O people of Dingri, those who brandish the spear of aware-
    ness within the state of emptiness
are unhindered[159] in their view of reality.[160]

This method of searching for the mind is also the intent of the
great Indian treatises. As the bodhisattva Shantideva[161] has said,

Without some sense of the thing being imagined
there is no apprehension of its unreality.[162]

And *Introduction to the Middle Way* states:

Through discernment, yogis realize that all of the faults and
    afflictions
arise from the view that thinks of the perishable aggregates[163]
    as a real person;
and once they have understood the self that is the object of
    that mind,
they uproot the [false notion of] self.[164]

And also:

The sages have taught that every instance of reversing
    misconception
is the fruit of analysis.[165]

b. The revelation of the actual primordial nature of mind through the identification of the three bodies of a buddha

By engaging in the type of analysis explained above, one ascertains that all phenomena that belong to the three categories—samsara, nirvana, and the path—have no real, objective foundation and lack any ground, that they are primordially pure emptiness, lacking true existence. When this is ascertained, because, in the first instance, they arise from nowhere, the mind's own nature lacks any intrinsic arising; this is the Dharma body (*dharmakaya*). Because, in the middle instance, they abide nowhere, there is a naked, non-grasping awareness that is empty and clear; this is the enjoyment body (*sambhogakaya*). And in the final instance, even though they go nowhere, there are emanation bodies (*nirmanakaya*), the creative radiance that unceasingly manifests [in various forms throughout the universe]. The basis for accomplishing the three bodies is the "three bodies as ground," which exist intrinsically within each of us. Those three bodies as ground are recognized through the "three bodies as path," the master's instructions, and through melding the mother and son.[166] [386] As the *Clear Expanse*[167] states:

> When you do not find a source for the mind,
> you resolve that the mind's nature is empty.
> That emptiness, devoid of apprehended object,
> is recognized as the Dharma body.

And also:

> Emptiness devoid of any conceptual identifications
> is recognized as the body of perfect enjoyment,
> which is also recognized as empty and yet unceasing.

And finally:

> The mind's nature, its lack of arising and ceasing,
> is recognized as the emanation body.
> In this way the three bodies are completely contained within
>   the mind.

Settle single-pointedly into the nature and essence of mind [understood] in this way; settle into the fact that it in no way exists ultimately. As the *Mound of Jewels Sutra*[168] states:

> Kashyapa, the mind does not exist inside you; nor does it exist outside; nor both. It cannot be perceived. The mind lacks form. It cannot be shown. It is nonmaterial. Even the buddhas have not perceived the mind; they do not perceive it now; nor will they ever perceive it in the future.[169]

And Shantideva, the child of the Conqueror, states:

> The mind does not reside within the sense organs and so on,
> nor is it something found in matter and so on,
>   nor is it somewhere between [the organs and the objects
>   they perceive].
> The mind is not internal, nor is it external,
> nor is it found anywhere else [apart from these two options].
> It is not something corporeal, nor is it elsewhere than in the
>   body.
> It is not a mixture [of material and nonmaterial factors], nor
>   is it something separate from these.

It is none of these things, and that is why

the essence of mind is nirvana.[170]

Therefore, when the conceptual thought "all phenomena are empty" occurs to you, look at the nature of the mind that is thinking that thought. Understanding that that mind *too* lacks any intrinsic existence, settle into that state. How do you settle therein? You do so by settling into a lucidly clear, nonconceptual state in which there is no apprehension of the ultimate nonexistence of anything at all by any mind whatsoever.

c. A somewhat more elaborate explanation of how to maintain the aspect of meditative stability so as to attain firmness in regard to the primordial mind

(A) An explanation of the three aspects of stabilizing meditation on mind, and how experience progressively arises in the adept[171]

The concentration-aspect of such a practice successively gives rise to small, medium, and great experiences. The first type of experience occurs when there is only a small level of mental stability. The experience [of the novice meditator] is like a mountain waterfall. When a conceptual thought arises [387], its nature is seen right away, and it is self-liberated. But immediately thereafter thoughts and concepts begin to erupt, and one is unable to stabilize the mind for any length of time; the analogy is a waterfall plunging from the side of a mountain. The lord Zhepa Dorjé [i.e., Milarepa] states:

Focusing one's attention on the internal workings of
the mind,

its impermanence—like the [fluttering wings of the] *shingkha*
bird—becomes manifest.
Not resting anywhere for even a single instant, it flies away.
Have you attained conviction of mind's nature,
      Rechungpa?[172]

When the mind first comes to rest, conceptual thoughts seem to
arise one after another, and you may think, "Meditation is caus-
ing *more* conceptualization to occur." The feeling that more conceptual thoughts are arising actually means that you have found a
bit of mental stability. In actuality, your previous conceptions are
just as they were before you started meditating, only before you
were unaware of the movement of the conceptual mind. As Zhang
Rinpoché[173] states:

> When stability first arises,
> it is like a waterfall plunging from a steep mountain:
> conceptions emerge without interruption.
> It may occur to you, "I have no meditative experience."
> But that feeling that there is an increase in conceptual
>   activity
> actually means that consciousness has attained a bit of
>   stability.
> The conceptual mind is operating just as before
> when there was no stability.
> Only then, when conceptual thoughts arose, you were not
>   aware of them.[174]

When conceptual thoughts suddenly arise, you remain naturally
relaxed and rest just so. By doing this again and again, you will come

to nakedly witness the clear-light nature of mind so that during the moment between one conceptual thought and the next, you come to rest the mind for a little while into its own nature. You then sustain your relaxed attention on the nature of the mind without becoming distracted by thought, and by so doing, the unrelenting waves of gross conceptual thoughts are pacified as a matter of course. This is the medium level of mental stability, a form of mental stability that is like the Ganges River gently flowing downstream. As Lama Zhang describes it:

> Then consciousness slows down, conceptualization
>   decreases,
> and the mind becomes like a gently flowing river.

At this point, no matter what appears when the mind is scattered from its nature, you remain firm without being distracted by thoughts until such time as whatever appears arises vividly in the mind as something that is groundless and lacking in any foundation. Doing this brings about insight into the nature of the primordial state. As the lord Maitripa[175] states,

> Until you cut the root of mind,
>   do not allow consciousness to be carefree.

Marpa puts it this way:

> Realization is by nature instantaneous.
> Once it suddenly happens, there is nothing to add or
>   subtract from it.

This is self-liberation, the great bliss of the primordial
   state.
Being free of hopes and worries is the result.[176]

And Lord Milarepa states:

Although this conceptual chatter of the mind does arise,
it is unborn, without foundation, and groundless.
Confidence undistracted by thought [388] is necessary.
Has certainty about this entered your mind, Rechungpa?[177]

And the incomparable Yang Gönpa[178] says:

The seeds of having accustomed yourself to bad thoughts
   are like a paper scroll [that constantly rolls itself up];
even when you generate new spiritual experiences, other conditions destroy them.
Because error is not eliminated in just a short time,
prolong your meditation, all you fortunate ones.

By practicing in this way, gross conceptual thoughts will not over-
whelm you. Then, as you rest in this limited bodily and mental
bliss, increase the meditation period. Zhang Rinpoché thinks that,
once this has been accomplished, *mental stability* refers to the state
in which:

Finally, consciousness becomes stable and does not move,
like the water in the depths of the ocean.

The final [experience of stability is likened unto] "an eel slithering without stirring the ocean." But do not become attached to states of bliss. As Lord Milarepa states:

> Do not savor the experiences of bliss
> that come about due to the waning of gross conceptual
>   thoughts
> within the waves of contaminated happiness.[179]

And also:

> Don't conceive of yourself as having attained the sublime
>   state
> when your meditation is just based on nonconceptual calm
>   abiding (*shamatha*).[180]

When you engage in the practice of mental stability in this way, you first try to accomplish mental steadiness. When you try to achieve this, if you are impeded by mental dullness and excitation, there are methods of meditation that can serve as antidotes. You should do as Urgyen Rinpoché himself taught:

> In reponse to dullness, awareness needs to be invigo-
> rated and made wide awake; meditate on making it
> expansive as if it were like space. In response to mental
> excitation, awareness needs to be dampened; meditate
> on impermanence and the suffering of samsara to shake
> the mind. If you become scattered, look upon the very
> nature of that scattering and meditate by holding tightly
> onto the object of your meditation. If dullness overtakes

you, pray to your spiritual master. Lift up your awareness and meditate on things that bring joy to the mind.
If your mind becomes diffuse, hold on to it tightly with
self-discipline. Reel it in completely. Focusing your eyes
on the tip of your nose, stare nakedly upon your own
nature. The mental diffusion is thereby dispelled.

So if the mind becomes too loose in the way it holds the object,
think, "I am experiencing mental dullness," and invigorate your
awareness. Then think, "If I continue to tighten my control, either
my mind will stray to another thought or else I will experience
mental excitation." As a result, you relax the control, and without
forcing it any further, you experience a balanced state. This is how
you should understand the way to cultivate the nature of mind
through analysis [of the level of one's concentration].

Now there is an alternative method of eliminating mental dullness and excitation that confronts these obstacles head on and
makes them a part of the path.[181] Do as Urgyen Rinpoché states:

Have trust in the method that does not look upon mental dullness and excitation as faults.[182]

Dampa Rinpoché also alludes to this when he states:

If mental dullness occurs, I dispell it using the syllable *pé*
(*phat*).
If mental scattering occurs, I cut it at the root.
If mental excitation occurs, I place it in the sphere of
reality.[183]

And the Lord Zhepa Dorjé says:

> As soon as the mind becomes excited, trample on it with the
> view. [389]
> The mind is thereby self-liberated from signs. How utterly
> amazing![184]

Or else do as Yang Gönpa says:

> When dullness and lethargy cloud the mind, visualize the
> master on top of the meeting point of the three channels
> at the forehead;[185]
> and if mental excitation occurs, visualize him or her [where
> the three channels meet] below the navel.

So when mental dullness or excitation occurs, meditate on the spiritual master at these two places on your body. Because this is a proper method, it is also permissible to meditate on the fact that the subtle drop located at those two places is of the nature of your spiritual master. Lord Dromtönpa[186] also teaches an antidote to mental scattering and excitation when he states:

> Relax consciousness within the place of the storm, and it
> becomes a virtue.

(B) An explanation of how, based on that, the nature of realization arises

Once you have rid yourself of mental dullness and excitation by practicing in this way, your whole mind is resting on its mental object. Nonetheless, subtle conceptualizations still move through the mind. When they do, do not resort to modifying your meditation by using antidotes. Do not even look upon those conceptual thoughts as faults, but rather just allow the conceptual thoughts[187] to settle in a relaxed way into their natural state. By so doing, the uncontrived nature of the primordial state—the clear light devoid of [dualisms like] "meditation object" and "meditating agent"— arises starkly. The insight that results from such an experience is called "seeing the nature of mind." It is also called "the recognition of the primordial state, the innate gnosis" as well as "the experience of the Dharma body of the basis clear light." As Tilopa[188] states:

> *Kye ho!* This is the gnosis of self-awareness.
> It is beyond speech and is not an object of thought.
> I, Tilopa, have nothing to teach.
> Know the self-symbolized state by yourself.[189]

And the Lord Götsangpa[190] states:

> Just by virtue of being human, our consciousness
> exists as the Dharma body.
> Although the master points to it, this is not necessary,
> for it is already present in one's own mind.[191]

Lord Milarepa also states:

> In between one conceptual thought and the next,
> gnosis continuously arises. Go taste it!

Longchenpa's *Treasury of Reality* states:

> No matter how the mind fluctuates, settle naturally into the
> natural state.
> The meaning of reality becomes clear within the very move-
> ment and scattering of thought.[192]

Lingrepa[193] states:

> The Lord [Milarepa] said, "Meditate on the meaning of the
> primordial state!"
> But when you meditate you must do away with
> notions of "meditation object" and "meditating agent" until
> they disappear.
> Guess what? There is no such thing as a division into medi-
> tation sessions and breaks!

This is the same point made by Lord Marpa when he states:

> I understood this inner-fixated mental consciousness
> to be the mind's essence recognizing itself,
> like meeting an old friend.
> Like the dream dreamed by a person who cannot speak,
> I had an experience that was inexpressible. [390]
> I understood the one meaning that cannot be put into words,
> just as a youth experiences happiness.[194]

(c) Eliminating doubts concerning the differences between three [states of mind]: resting/stillness (*né*[195]), mental fluctuations (*gyu*[196]), and awareness (*rig*[197])

Former masters have said that at the time of these experiences, one can distinguish between three degrees of mental fluctuations: subtle, somewhat gross, and very coarse. For example, among the various states of mind that engage in virtuous practices, the thought to quench one's thirst [while continuing to practice virtue] is a subtle fluctuation. The thought that forgets about the practice of virtue and thinks only to quench one's thirst is somewhat rough. And actually engaging in the action of quenching one's thirst through an act of body and speech is a very coarse fluctuation. If [what these former masters have said] is so, then all three types of fluctuations must be fluctuations that occur only in the context of a beginner's practice of stabilizing meditation.

But I myself believe that only the *very coarse* fluctuations occur during a beginner's stabilizing meditation, in which there is a continuous flow of conceptualization. I believe that *somewhat rough* fluctuations occur in the context of the second stage of stillness, where the mind, resting quietly on its object, is suddenly disturbed by a conceptual thought, like a fish leaping out of water. And finally, I believe that *subtle fluctuations* occur when one is expertly concentrated, when one is resting single-pointedly on the nature of mind. In this latter case, even though subtle conceptualization is occurring, the mind finds its own way back to a state of natural repose, like a camel that is tied to a stone and allowed to wander off.

Well then, in this [latter state, when the mind is still and at rest], do fluctuations occur while one is meditating and concentrated? And is there stillness or not during the fluctuations?

Some of my own expert masters claim that such a [simultaneity of stillness and fluctuations] is impossible. But if this is so, is the impossibility [of the simultaneity of stillness and fluctuations] the unique position of the seminal essence (*nyingtig*) tradition, or is this a position held in common by both the Mahamudra and Dzogchen traditions? It is difficult to claim that the first option is correct. If we maintained that, it would lead to a confusion regarding the context, for we must remember that the present context is one in which we are identifying the general and pervasive view that is the common intention of all three great traditions.[198] The second option—[that it is a view held only in the Mahamudra and Dzogchen traditions, and is not found, for example, in the broader Madhyamaka tradition]—is also not correct, for Saraha states:

> If you let go of the mind bound by ordinary mental
>   concerns,
> there is no doubt that you will be free.[199]

And Urgyen Rinpoché states:

> No matter which of the conceptual thoughts of the five poi-
>   sons may arise—
> the afflictions that move toward their mental objects—
> do not engage in any mental artifice, either anticipating them
>   or following after them.
> Instead, allowing the mental fluctuations to settle into their
>   own state, one is liberated into the Dharma body.[200]

This implies that stillness can occur *during* the fluctuations. And, once again, Padmasambhava states:

> Do not see the various disturbances of awareness that occur
>   during the son's path
> as either faults or virtues. Instead, meet them head-on, and
>   incorporate them into the path.[201] [391]

And also:

> By concentrating on the meaning of the letter *hum,*
> my mind enters into the great space of reality; and from that
>   state
> awareness suddenly arises on its own in a single instant.

This is telling us that fluctuations exist *while the mind is still.* There-fore, within the present context, it seems to me a contradiction to accept on the one hand that conceptual thoughts are the Dharma body and to accept on the other that it is impossible for there to be stillness while there are mental fluctuations. But this should be examined in greater detail.

   This position [that a still mind can be subject to fluctuations and vice versa] is not unique to the seminal essence tradition, for *The Clear Expanse* [a text that predates the seminal essence compila-tion?] states:

> The mind that grasps at things dualistically
> arises from the six objects of clear gnosis.

So fluctuations *can* exist while there is stillness. Once again, Longchenpa states:

No matter how the mind fluctuates, settle naturally into the
natural state.
The meaning of reality becomes clear within the very movement and scattering of thought.[202]

So there can be mental stillness even while one is experiencing
fluctuations.

(D) **An explanation of the differences between how three
states—stillness (*nepa*[203]), experiences (*nyamnyong*[204]), and
realizations (*togpa*[205])—arise for three types of individuals**
During the three degrees of meditative stability—low, intermediate, and highest—what are the differences in how the three types
of individuals—the instantaneous type (*chigcharwa*[206]), the skipping
type (*tögelwa*[207]), and the gradual type (*rimgyipa*[208])—give rise to experiences and realization?[209]

Gradualists first achieve the three stages of mental stillness; only
then do experiences arise for them, and only after experiences does
realization fully arise. As Zhang Rinpoché states:

This is how the three arise for the gradualist:
First, only a slight stillness arises;
then experiences arise in a definitive way;[210]
then realization fully arises.
When the first sign of stillness arises...

And at the end of the previously cited lines, he states:

Finally, their consciousness rests firmly and without wavering, like the water in the depths of the ocean;

then experiences arise

like the center of a pure sky,

and they feel a bliss that is clear and nonconceptual.

This is stating that gradualists first go through the three stages of stillness, and only *then* do they have an experience of bliss. How does realization dawn for them? Again, Zhang Rinpoché states:

When Mahamudra yogis

relax consciousness,

there arises an experience of clarity that is nonconceptual,

like the center of a pure sky.

When such a state arises,

they ascertain the immeasurable extent of their sins and

obscurations.

Although an ascertaining consciousness is not actually

generated,

they come into contact with the Dharma body.

When the realization of innate nonduality

fully arises for them,

in a single instant, and without any impediment, [392]

all of the sins they have accumulated since beginningless time

are utterly destroyed.

For the *skipping* type, it is realization that arises first, but that realization is unstable. Therefore, for them there is no fixed order to the three—experience, realization, and mental stillness—and that is why they are called the *skipping type*. Once again, Zhang Rinpoché states:

This is how they arise for the skipping type:
From among the three states—stillness, experience, and
    realization—
realization fully arises first.
But although they realize the truth, this understanding is
    unstable, like waves that come and go.
Sometimes they enter into experiences and sometimes into
    stillness.
There is no fixed pattern.
The degree of their experience is the play of awareness.

For individuals of the *instantaneous* type, as soon as the master
has given them the pointing-out instructions,[211] or else based on
those instructions, all three states arise simultaneously without
their needing to meditate on the naked experience, realization, or
stillness that rests on the nature of mind. This is how it happens:
the moment that they see or realize the nature of the uncontrived,
primordial state, their minds achieve a full and naked stillness that
rests on that nature, and there arises for them the bliss of such an
experience—all three qualities occurring instantaneously. As Zhang
Rinpoché states:

As for individuals of the instantaneous type,
as soon as a master who possesses the essence of realization
reveals the instructions to them,
or else simply through the mind's mere gaze,
the three states—experience, realization, and stillness—
arise all at once without their having to meditate.
Although experiences may increase or decrease,
their realization remains stable and unchanging.

Although monkeys run up and down the tree,
the tree remains stable and unchanging.

2. Having identified [the innate primordial state], how to engage in the practice
a. An explanation of how to practice this both in the state of meditative equipoise and in the aftermath [i.e., post-equipoise] state
(A) The brief explanation

There are two different methods: (1) one in which the meditative equipoise is like space and the aftermath consciousness[212] is like a harvest[213] and (2) one in which the meditative state is like space and the aftermath state is like an illusion. Here is the difference, according to Chetsangpa Rinchen Peljor:[214]

Externally, there is no fixation on objects.
Internally, awareness is clear and vivid.
This outer and inner transparency of awareness
is the *meditative equipoise*, Ane Ma.

When one is slightly distracted from that state,
there is a sudden movement toward objects.
That misty appearance of subject-object duality
is the *aftermath consciousness*, Ane Ma.

Then, forcefully [393] holding on to awareness with
    mindfulness,
the conception of subject and object becomes self-pacified,
and then the previous equipoise is revitalized.
This is the *aftermath state*, Ane Ma.

And he explains:

> Continuous and relaxed stability on the instructions is
> called *experience.*[215] From that state, good and bad con-
> ceptions occur based on the appearance of the six types
> of sense objects. But no matter what conceptions arise,
> one forcefully focuses on one's own nature without
> trying to alter those conceptions by accepting some
> and discarding others. Having relaxed into the natu-
> ral state, one settles therein, as a result of which the
> conceptions are released into the self-liberated state.
> When this occurs, anything that appears becomes an
> aid to meditation. When the aftermath consciousness
> has been incorporated into the path, this is called the
> *aftermath state.*[216]

When one finds the aspect of stillness in regard to the mind, from
within the great bliss of the primordial state, devoid of thought
and expression, without following after any conception that may
arise, one enters nonconceptually into single-pointed equipoise on
the nature of consciousness that is at ease, relaxed, fresh, and free.
This is what in this system is known as *equipoise.* If you lose the perch
of mindfulness, and conceptions suddenly arise, you pay them no
heed, as a result of which it is said that there occurs an *aftermath
consciousness* that is like a harvest, or an *aftermath state* that has not yet
been incorporated into the path. After rising from that equipoise,
every object of the six senses that appears to you appears as an illusion; it appears as the indivisible play of bliss and emptiness, and
as the union of appearance and emptiness. When even the appearance of objects acts as an aid to equipoise, it is called "an aftermath

consciousness that has been incorporated into the path" and "the
aftermath state in which things appear as an illusion." As the Lord
Marpa states:

> The appearance of objects grasped as external things
> was cut off within the state of great bliss,
> and I realized them to be the unborn Mahamudra.[217]

And the Lord Milarepa states:

> Whatever appears, whether internal or external,
> appears erroneously during nonrealization periods,
> and attachment to objects during this time causes bondage.
> Within periods of realization, things appear as illusions,
> and the appearance of objects serves as an aid to the mind.
> In the final stage, one does not experience appearances at all.
> This is called "purification into the unborn Dharma body."

It is true that the terminology "the aftermath consciousness like a
harvest" and "aftermath state where things appear like an illusion"
is little known. But terminology like "aftermath consciousness that
has or has not incorporated appearances into the path" is known
among Mahamudra and Dzogchen yogis like Yang Gönpa, who
use these notions in a way similar to those [first two lesser-known
terms].

Let me now put the practice of the equipoise and aftermath
states in a concise form. Instantly recall your usual root master
and pray to him. [394] Do not analyze the tracks of past conceptions. Do not anticipate the future.[218] Ask yourself, "What am I

conceiving precisely in this present moment? How is this shifting in my mind?" and then stare nakedly at the very moment of your present conceptual thought. By so doing, the movement of conceptions is completely undermined, and until you become distracted again, conceptions do not occur. When you *do* become distracted and conceptions abruptly arise, by staring nakedly at the very conceptions that emerge, you approach the state of nonconceptuality with equilibrium. In this way, whatever conceptions arise, you accept them and you look directly at them.[219]

Do not make your sessions very long; increase their clarity[220] and do away with distraction, making your sessions short in duration but frequent in number. By following this procedure over and over again, when you have been able to recognize your conceptions for one two-hour period,[221] you will be free from them. What does it mean to recognize conceptions? It means to directly generate a consciousness that ascertains that conceptions are unborn, unceased, unabiding, unreal, ungraspable, and like the sky. That point is also called the "mixing of experience and realization into a single whole." It is with reference to this that Gampo Dawö Zhönnu[222] said:

> Because this conception, unarisen in terms of any attribute,
> is the Dharma body, it is directly apprehended.[223]

(B) **The extensive explanation**
(*1*) **How to practice in the state of equipoise**
(*a*) **How to meditate on calm abiding**
(i) **How to cultivate mindfulness so as to elicit the five contacts without having to place the mind into a dormant state**
Without being distracted even for an instant, rest in the nature of

mind, holding it tight with discipline just as you would when put-
ting a thread through the eye of a needle; then rest on that without
even the least mental movement. If the session seems to drag on,
slightly loosen [your grip on the object] from time to time, but do
not lose the practice of mindfulness that keeps the mind in contact
[with the object]. As Yang Gönpa states:

> [Hold fast to the object] like an only son longing for his
>   dead mother:[224]
> constantly, without forgetting it, and without distraction.

So do not allow yourself to be distracted even for an instant. When
you possess such undistracted mindfulness, there arises a vigilance
that [monitors the level of the mind and] is barely aware when the
mind is slightly distracted or undistracted. As *Entering the Bodhisattva
Practice* states:

> Once you have stabilized the mind on the object being con-
>   templated, [395]
> through the use of mindfulness,
> vigilance will come.[225]

And *Six Verses on Yoga*[226] states:

> Vigilance is a concomitant mental factor of mindfulness.
> It is a knowledge that understands[227] the subtle states of the
>   mind:
> whether or not the faults of mental dullness and excitation
>   are occurring.

(ii) How to let the mind go into its natural state so as to still it without the binding action of effort

Saraha states:

> Brahman, just like spinning thread,
> the yogi should rest the mind through loosening it.[228]

So you cultivate the natural state of the mind itself in a peaceful, easy, relaxed state without the slightest distraction, and without forgetting the object even slightly. As Zhang Rinpoché states:

> Like a raven that has flown from the ship,[229]
> Do not re-collect the scattered mind onto the object.
> Like a butter lamp undisturbed by the wind,
> Rest in clarity without conceptualization and without
>   distraction.
> Like the fire that engulfs a forest,
> Allow whatever appears to settle into the Great Seal.
> Like the stars and constellations reflecting on the ocean,
> Allow phenomenal appearances to settle into the Great Seal.
> Like an expert herds his cattle,
> The yogi lets consciousness do as it pleases.[230]

So by loosening the mind within a state that is nondistracted, keep your sessions moderate and meditate so as to increase their clarity. As Urgyen Rinpoché states:

> Free your meditation again and again without becoming
>   attached to it.[231]

And also:

> Whatever conceptions arise, whether good or bad, confront
> them directly.
> Short sessions, but many in number, like water dripping in
> an empty house.
> Do not coerce the body and mind but allow them to settle
> loosely and easily.[232]

Having engaged in a detailed interrogation of all of those points,
ask yourself whether you have understood the meditation and how
it is that progress occurs.[233]

At this point, with a proper posture, and having gone through
the physical exercises, as soon as you have begun to meditate on
the mind, the conceptions cease by being pacified into their natural
state. Having been pacified into their natural state, the mind is automatically relaxed into nonconceptuality. Abiding single-pointedly
in that state is what this system calls *meditation*.

(b) How to meditate on insight
(i) The revelation of the true face of reality, and identifying
the Dharma body through naked vision of the truth

Rid yourself of any notion of yourself as "the meditator," and
even of any thoughts like "I am meditating." Do not even have
a notion of "what I am meditating on." Do not meditate while
holding on to any thoughts like "bliss," "clarity," "nonconceptuality," and so forth. Not thinking of anything whatsoever,
the mind settled automatically into its natural state, do not
allow yourself to be distracted. This is not mental dullness, for

awareness will be meditatively engaged in an alert and wakeful way. This is not mental excitation, [396] for you will not be entertaining any conceptions, neither of the past nor of the future. You are in equipoise. When clarity has been maintained throughout the session, cut off discursivity and meditate. By meditating single-pointedly in this way, all the phenomena that belong to the category of phenomenal appearances do not lose their self-glow.²³⁴ When, without objects changing their hue, the self-arisen innate gnosis, the primordial Mahamudra arises— when there nakedly arises without objectification the nature of self-luminous, present consciousness that, while not having any fixed nature, does not block the radiance [of the world]—this is called the *arising of realization*. It is also what in this teaching is referred to as the *birth of the sprout of insight*. It is also known as *directly seeing the primordial mind*. This is what *The Testament*²³⁵ is referring to when it says:

> This awareness, which cannot be fixed as being anything
>   in particular,
> is self-appearing, while at the same time not obstructing the
>   way that things appear.
> All phenomenal appearances at this point arise as the uni-
>   verse of the Dharma body.
> That appearance is liberated into its own state.

And the *Sixth Expanse* states:

> Within the inexpressible nature of mind,
> calm abiding and insight arise on their own.

> That is why the nature of mind is perfected as the
>   unwavering meditative state
> within both equipoise and its aftermath.[236]

And the Lord Dagpo Lhajé [i.e., Gampopa] also states that the coemergence of the nature of mind is as follows. First, without thoughts of effort and goal, you deeply relax the body and mind. In the middle, you lose your doubts, and so the mind rests in an uncontrived natural state. In the end, all sensations will be understood as being unborn.

Having practiced in this way, you witness the nature of the primordial state. What is this like? The Lord Dagpo Lhajé asks, "What does the term *primordial state* mean?" He answers that it does not hold on to any base. It does not impede any possibilities. It does not fall into any fixed positions. It does not fixate on any long-term goals. It cannot be signified through any example. It is not something that comes to you by means of any words.

This is what he means: "In the first instance, it does not hold on to any base" means that it does not depend on any consciousness, unlike the example of the pigeon [who requires a perch]. "It does not impede any possibilities" means that it is devoid of hoping for, entertaining doubts about, abandoning, or achieving anything. "It does not fall into any fixed positions" means that it does not fall into the extremes of eternalism and nihilism. "It does not fixate on any long-term goals" means that it is devoid of desire. "It cannot be signified through any example" means that it is devoid of being identifiable in any way. "It is not something that comes to you by means of any words" means that it is beyond all expression. [397]

Such a primordial mind can only be realized through the blessing of the compassionate master. As the *Hevajra Tantra*[237] states:

> The state cannot be expressed by anyone else, but arises
>   spontaneously.
> It is not something that can be acquired in any way.
> It can be known only by relying on the master's timely
>   interventions
> and is the result of one's own merit.[238]

And Dagpo Rinpoché states that it is something that arises in the
religious lineage of a master who possesses the eye of the doctrine
and who has realization. When disciples have the proper faith and
devotion, they realize it, and it comes to them. If the master lacks
realization, then it does not matter if the disciples have faith and
devotion.[239] For example, if a mold[240] has no design in it, then no
matter how good the lump of clay, the molded sculpture will not
take shape. If the disciples have no faith and devotion, it does not
matter that the master possesses the instructions. It is like the case
of a cow who has rich milk but whose calf [cannot suckle because
it] has no palate.

Even in these advanced contexts, you still intermittently practice
the previously explained instructions on searching for the mind.
In the context of all such practices, you must not discard the cultivation of the three things: (1) the recollection of impermanence,
which brings an urgency to life, (2) conviction in karmic cause and
effect, and (3) the generation of love, compassion, and the mind
directed to enlightenment. The Lord Dagpo Lhajé states that this
is why the stages of the path (*lamrim*) are valued so highly. If you do

not possess [these foundational teachings] within your mind, even if a glimmer of the primordial state is generated in your mind, you become attached to things, to relatives, to wealth, and to possessions, in which case the primordial state is of no use to you. You go down instead of up. Therefore, do not become attached to this life. Since all phenomena—sights and sounds—are like illusions and dreams, let the mind enter into this truth. Practice love, compassion, and the altruistic mind of enlightenment. The one who ascertains such truths will only go up and not down. Lord Milarepa states:

> Since it is only death that makes me shudder,
> I have trained in the deathless primordial state.

And the glorious Pagmodrupa[241] states:

> If you remember death and impermanence—that you are like an animal destined for slaughter—at first, your mind turns toward the doctrine. In the middle, the doctrine turns toward the path. And at the end, you obtain the Mahamudra of the clear light.

Lama Zhang likewise states:

> How great it is to have trained in a way that causes you
>   to take
> love, compassion, and the altruistic mind of enlightenment
>   as the center of your practice of the path.
> Nothing profits you more.

> Eventually, the nondiscursive state [398] arises as great
> compassion.
> The grasping of things as true is released into the space of
> the nondiscursive state
> that lacks any ground or essence, and the desiring agent is
> liberated.

Once the true face of reality has been revealed to you by these methods, from time to time go over the material by asking questions, and gain certainty about the state to which you have been introduced, doing this in such a way that you resolve the leftover, unresolved points.

(ii) Identifying one's own nature while the mind is in motion, and showing how whatever arises is simultaneously liberated

As above, contemplate without distraction the nature of the primordial mind, the innate gnosis. There are no differences whatsoever—good, bad, or otherwise—between the two states: (1) when various conceptions are being projected out of the mind and (2) when the mind is stabilized and not engaged in such projections. No matter what conceptions sway you, their nature is nothing but mind. For example, various things, like clouds, arise within space. When they arise, they arise from space; when they disappear, they disappear into the expanse of space; and when they remain, they remain within the expanse of space. Likewise, when conceptions are projected out, they are projected out of the mind; when they disappear, they disappear into the mind; and when they abide, they abide within the mind. Like the center of clear space, the nature of those conceptions, as this is experienced by yogis, cannot be expressed. Longchenpa makes this same point when he states:

> When scattering occurs, the "scatterer" is the mind;
> lacking color and shape, it cannot be pinned down.
> When it rests, the "rester" is the mind;
> it is the primordial reality that is liberated from the start.
> There is nothing to accept or reject, no hopes or worries, no judgments.
> One just settles into the great foundationless state that is empty from the start.

The nature of mind, empty and having no self, gives rise to good and bad conceptions due to the bad predispositions that are the result of having accustomed oneself to error; but when these conceptions arise, they are just the mind. By looking directly into the nature of what arises, conceptions are pacified into their own state, and you enter into emptiness; but when this happens, it *too* is just the mind. No matter what is projected, and no matter how these projections move, their nature is nothing other than the mind. Therefore, whatever appears is recognized as traceless and inconceivable. It is with this in mind that Lord Milarepa said:

> Hey you! It's easy to meditate on the nature of mind.
> Conceptions are the mind's magical apparitions.
> Although they occur, they arise from the mind itself.
> Although they vanish, they vanish into the mind itself.
> So just rest in the mind's own nature.

And also:

> When conceptions exist within the mind, [399]
> hold on to your own mind with the hook of mindfulness.
> Rest in a state of equipoise
> without grasping at samsara and nirvana as two different
>   things.
> Sustain yourself in the state of equality in which anything
>   that appears is seen as traceless.

Practice in this way.

(2) How to practice in the aftermath state
(a) Recognizing that appearances are mind

In the state of meditative equipoise, there arises an ascertaining consciousness that cuts through reification, but in the aftermath state any phenomenon that appears to the mind, whether it belongs to samsara or to nirvana—and in particular, any external appearance that arises, such as form, sound, and so on—appears to be independent, self-sustaining, and concrete. But these are only the appearances of the latent potentials of the error of dualistic grasping. They lack even the slightest bit of true existence. Hence, while they are appearing, you relax the mind and let it come to rest. When you do this, things appear nakedly as the indivisible union of appearance and emptiness, and this is what is called "the state in which appearances possess the carefree nature of the Dharma body." It means the same thing as "identifying appearances as empty" and "identifying appearances as mind." As Tilopa states:

Appearances do not bind you; conceptual attachments
   bind you.
Cut off conceptual attachments, Naropa.[242]

And also:

I know the state in which appearances possess the carefree
   nature of the Dharma body
by relaxing mind in regard to external objects

And Götsangpa[243] states:

This is known as "cultivating a carefree state in regard
to appearances."[244]

For example, depending on the beholder, a single individual may appear as beautiful, as ugly, or as average-looking, but this does not contradict the fact that it is one and the same individual who is being seen. Likewise, even though these appearances appear in different ways, as objects they are equal insofar as they are unborn. In brief, whatever appears is empty, and what is empty arises as bliss. Hence, you should see everything as the shimmering play of the indivisibility of bliss and emptiness. As Saraha states:

Just as unperturbed waters turn into turbulent waves
when they are agitated by wind,
likewise you, O King, create diversity in regard to the image
   of the archer [Saraha]
even though there is only a unity here.
Just as the deluded see a single lamp as two

due to having faulty vision,

likewise, there is no distinction between the seer and the seen.

How amazing, then, that the mind should give rise to

dualities.[245]

This is telling us that all phenomena share a nondual equality. Therefore, to say that "appearances are your own mind" not only means that all appearances can only be posited on the basis of being imputed by the mind or by consciousness, it also means that "they lack true existence." [400] The meaning of the above quotes is *not* similar to the Mind-Only school's [idealism].

(*b*) Recognizing conceptions as the Dharma body

(i) The "Dharma body of conceptions at the level of the basis," which, whether or not it is understood, is the Dharma body, like the example of a treasure buried inside the house of a poor person[246]

The *Hevajra Root Tantra* states:

Sentient beings are enlightened,

but this enlightened state is obscured by adventitious
stains.

When those stains have been eliminated, beings are
buddhas.[247]

This is stating that the primordial mind that exists in the mental continuum of sentient beings is the basis for accomplishing the Dharma body of a buddha. In the *Dohas* we find:

"Erring on account of not seeing the nature of the primordial state,
the childish are deceived." So says the archer.[248]

This is stating that ordinary beings err because they fail to notice
the primordial mind present within their ordinary consciousness.
As the master Nagarjuna states:

All beings lack freedom;
they are not born as free.
The cause of freedom is the clear light;
the clear light is the emptiness of all things.

This is stating that the clear light of death is the primordial mind,
following which he states:

That state of mind that has caused the childish
to be bound by the fetters of samsara
is the very state of mind
that leads the yogi to the state of buddhahood.

This is telling us that childish, ordinary beings circle around in
samsara because they do not recognize the innate gnosis of the
primordial mind of the clear light of death; and it is stating that
yogis accomplish the state of buddhahood by generating the states
whose nature is the analogue and actual clear light. So while it is
true that, at the level of the basis, the uncontrived primordial mind
of sentient beings never goes beyond conceptual thought, whether

or not yogis actually identify it as such, that gnosis inheres within each and every sentient being as the basis for accomplishing the Dharma body of a buddha. For example, a precious treasure hidden in the home of a poor person may not be recognized by the poor person himself or herself as a precious treasure. But it is nonetheless precious even while the person is poor [and unaware of the treasure's existence]. Having understood [that it is inside the house], it then does away with poverty, but even then that treasure does not go beyond its status as something precious. It is with this in mind that Lord Milarepa [401] states:

> That this is the fruit [of practice] is certain, but [whether
> you realize it] depends on your own mind.
> To search for the result elsewhere than in the mind
> is like abandoning the mind itself, O Physician.[249]

And the *Gnosis at the Moment of Death Sutra* states:

> When you realize the mind, this is gnosis. That is why you should meditate strongly on the recognition that buddhahood is not sought elsewhere than in the mind.[250]

The *Supreme Continuum*[251] and its commentaries explain these points in a more detailed fashion. In this context, one could also resort to recognizing [the buddha nature] through the example of the King Kang Khyampa.[252]

(ii) The "Dharma body of conceptions at the level of the path,"
which, given that conceptions that arise suddenly are now seen
to be Dharma body, is held on to forcefully
Lord Serlingpa[253] states:

> When they are distant, just relax.
> As they recede, stare nakedly at them.
> Settle quietly into the state of relaxation.
> This is how the fetters are set free.[254]

And as Lord Milarepa states:

> If conceptions do not appear as the Dharma body,
> how could they elicit a single instant of thought and
> perception?

And also:

> I, the yogi Milarepa,
> see the essence through naked staring.
> I see the lack of elaborations that is like the center of space.
> By settling directly on it, I realize reality.
> I realize all things to be by nature empty.
> By relaxing, I have grasped their natural state.
> The river of awareness is divided into the pure water and the
> scum.
> By utterly casting them aside, I cut off thoughts and
> conceptions.
> I have completely jumped over[255] the abyss of the six realms
> of beings.

So look at the nature of any of the conceptions that appear in your own mind. Pay them no heed and relax into the natural state. Once every sign has been pacified into its natural state, there arises a clear, empty, and naked awareness that is like the center of pure space. This is called "the appearance of conceptions as the Dharma body." It is with this in mind that the *Precious Book* states:

> Among all antidotes, which is supreme?
> The one that meets head on what is to be abandoned.
> What does it mean "to meet head on what is to be
>   abandoned"?
> It means to destroy an obstacle the very moment it arises.[256]

And Zhang Rinpoché states:

> When consciousness is relaxed,
> you experience a clarity that is nonconceptual.
> The mind appears like the center of a pure sky.
> That is the clear-light Dharma body.[257]

And also:

> To meditate on Mahamudra
> remain in a relaxed way during the thought process
> by discarding any precise notion about what is to be done.

Briefly, when, due to certain causes or conditions, any of the various good or bad conceptions suddenly arise, do not engage in any artificial measure. Rather, relax by letting the mind proceed into its natural state. Rest there without distraction or artifice. Gently give up thoughts in a carefree way. Once they have been naturally dispersed, [402] settle [into that relaxed state]. By so doing you practice in such a way that thoughts are liberated the very moment they arise. This is the "self-appearance and immediate self-liberation of all thoughts and conceptions," which is like a snake effortlessly uncoiling itself, and like drawing an image on water [something that immediately vanishes]. As Shavari[258] has stated:

When you understand your own nature for yourself,
even the distracted mind arises as Mahamudra.[259]

At that moment, you understand the self-nature of any conception that arises—for example, whatever good and bad appearances emerge as objects of the six groups of the senses. As a result of this, whatever thoughts arise are incorporated into the path. By realizing the unborn nature of the afflicted states of mind, you do not come under their influence, and so you do not accumulate karma. Because you master the practice of the view of emptiness, whatever conventional appearances arise—even while they appear to exist independently and concretely—from the very moment that they appear, they are known to be empty of true existence, to be lies, and to be like illusions. Like recognizing the fact that you have been deceived by a crafty companion, even though things appear, you have no conceptual attachments to them. All activities are seen to be like dreams and like illusions. Although empty, their appearing aspect is not blocked. Your body, appearing yet empty, stands proudly as the deity's body. Your voice, audible yet empty, arises as the recitation of the deity's mantra. And your mind, clear yet empty, grasping at nothing, rests in the union of emptiness and compassion. You should contemplate this without being distracted even for a moment. As the Lord Jigten Gönpo[260] states in his advice to Lord Chenngawa,[261]

> Without relying internally on the samadhi of great bliss,
> the body, speech, and mind become distracted externally.
> Because you have not been blessed by another's mindstream,
> I ask you to pour your mind into the water of clear
>   meditation.[262]

(iii) The "Dharma-body of conceptions at the level of result," which is like the stones that are not found on the Golden Isle

[The edition of the text at our disposal is missing this section.][263]

b. An explanation of the related instructions
(A) An exposition of the ground, path, and result

The expression "Mahamudra as the ground" refers to the fact that although all phenomena—those contained within the categories of appearance and existence and of samsara and nirvana—have never, from beginningless time, existed by virtue of their own nature, they nonetheless, at the conventional level, have the ability to perform their own functions, being of the nature of emptiness and dependent arising in such a way that these are inseparable. The expression "Mahamudra as path" refers to the cultivation of the experience of method and wisdom in union, an experience that takes place once one has cut through the reification of the "Mahamudra as ground." The expression "Mahamudra as result" refers to the actualization of the three bodies, the path's complete perfection of all that is to be abandoned and realized.

In what sense are these three states Mahamudra, the "Great Seal"? [403] They are called *mudra or* "seal" because there is no greater ground of all phenomena than this.[264] They are called *maha* or "great" because there is no reality above or superior to it, nothing that is more excellent, and this is because there is not a single one of the Buddha's good qualities missing within it.

(B) Identifying the specific characteristics of the path of the view, meditation, and action
(1) The real [path of view, meditation, and action]
[The view]

When you experience, or realize, Mahamudra as ground, you cut through reification. Hence when, using your own individual wisdom, you thoroughly examine any phenomenon belonging to either samsara or nirvana, there arises a wisdom or gnosis that understands the object without thinking that there is any phenomenon that exists by virtue of its own nature. This is what is called the "Mahamudra as view." As the *Hevajra Root Tantra* states:

> You see that there is no form that exists by its own
>   nature.
> There is no sound, and no one who hears.
> There is no scent, and no one who smells.
> There is no flavor, and no one who savors it.
> There is nothing touched, and no one who touches it.[265]

This passage is pointing to the nonexistence of the *self of phenomena*, from form up to touch and to the nonexistence of the *self of persons*, from "the one who sees" up to "the one who tastes." "By its own nature" is pointing to the fact that the kind of "self" that is lacking in both persons and phenomena is "existence by virtue of own nature." The *Condensed Verses on the Perfection of Wisdom* also states:

> When every phenomenon, whether composite or noncom-
>   posite, whether good or evil,
> is demolished by wisdom, so that not even the slightest bit
>   of it is perceived,
> this is what beings of the world reckon as the perfection of
>   wisdom.[266]

This is telling us that when one realizes that no phenomenon exists by virtue of its own nature, one has realized the meaning of emptiness, the direct teaching of the Perfection of Wisdom scriptures. Tilopa puts it this way:

> If you want to attain the state beyond thought, in which
>   there is nothing to be done,
> inquire into the foundations of your own mind and rest in
>   naked awareness.[267]

And Lord Milarepa states:

> No gods and no demons is what it means to trust in
>   the view.[268]

And also:

From the viewpoint of the ultimate truth,
  there's no such thing as buddhahood, much less such a thing
    as obstructing spirits.

A yogi who is chiefly engaged in the cultivation of such a view identifies the ground, path, and result based on a single moment of awareness. When this occurs, the unelaborated reality of the single moment of awareness that appears to the yogi is the ground. To understand its self-nature is the *view*. To settle the mind within the view is *meditation*. To make such a state into the path without ever letting it go is *action*. As Lord Atisha states:

Given that reality lacks elaborations,
  even consciousness rests in an unelaborated state.[269] [404]

To have actualized these [that is, the view, meditation, and action] is the effect. This is how these notions should be identified. It is with this in mind that Lord Milarepa states:

The uncontrived ground appears as the great omnipresent
    state.
The uncontrived path appears as the great unimpeded
    state.
The uncontrived effect appears as Mahamudra.

[Meditation]

"Mahamudra as meditation" refers to the fact that while "Mahamudra as view" is experiencing the nature of mind, one identifies and then meditates within a state of equipoise on the innate gnosis of the primordial mind so as to cut off reification.

[Action]

"Mahamudra as action" refers to the fact that, without letting go of the trust born from the view and meditation, one is motivated by the altruistic mind of enlightenment and trains in the discipline of the three vows that accord with one or another of the three levels of a vajra holder: superior, middling, or inferior.

(2) Cultivating the energy (*tsel*)²⁷⁰ [of the view, meditation, and action]

By practicing these three—view, meditation, and action—and having gained stability in regard to the altruistic mind of enlightenment, you train the energy so that it becomes unimpeded. We now explain this under two headings.

(a) The practice appropriate for beginners

After you have recognized the mind's own nature to be emptiness, conceptions and appearances continue to arise, but as soon as they appear, conceptual signs are experienced as if they were arising as an emptiness that liberates them into their natural state. Just as this experience is beginning, you engage in the enhancement practices from within that very experience.²⁷¹ It is said that for those of sharp faculties, this occurs even before one reaches the lowest stage of single-pointedness.²⁷² So you should meditate intensively [on the enhancement practices].

(*b*) The actual training of the energy that takes place on the higher paths

(i) Training the energy

During the stage of nonelaboration, one directly realizes the non-elaborated, empty nature of all phenomena. Nonetheless, in the aftermath state, the latent potentials that grasp at signs are strong. Therefore, it is said that while things are appearing, it is necessary to emphasize mindfulness in regard to the empty aspect of things; and by so doing it is said that even an aftermath consciousness that is not actually embraced by the equipoised view can arise. Therefore, during such times as things are appearing, be mindful of the fact that whatever appears is unborn, and through this mindfulness, train yourself, using the eight examples[273]—that everything that appears in the aftermath state is like an illusion. This is how you "train the energy." As Lord Atisha states:

> During the periods that follow the state of equipoise,
> accustom yourself to seeing all phenomena
> as being like the eight examples of illusory things.
> In such a way should you chiefly cultivate
> the view subsequent to equipoise and train in method.[274]

And the Gyalsé Rinpoché[275] states: ⌊405⌋

> There is no way to control the conceptions of the three poisons[276] during the aftermath state
> Without all thoughts and appearances arising as the dharma-body.
> So resort to mindfulness when you need it,

and do not give free rein to erroneous conceptions,
Maniwa.

Lord Milarepa states:

Soaring freely within the state of unborn mind,
the signs of birth and cessation are naturally pacified.
How delightful is such assurance about the view.

Train the energy as stated in these passages.

(ii) Mastery of the energy

During the time of the single taste, whatever appears appears without needing to rely on mindfulness of the unborn state. Whatever appears at this point arises as essential emptiness during its
very appearance. Therefore, when everything arises as the union
of appearance and emptiness without the deterioration of appearances, the energy has been mastered.

3. An explanation of how, having practiced this method, experiential realizations and the stages of spiritual development arise in the practitioner

a. The yoga of single-pointed concentration

All of the practices taught above are subsumed within the four
yogas.[277] This is because the four yogas are subsumed within the
five paths.[278] Now when a conceptual thought suddenly arises, you
relax and let the conception go without resorting to any artificial
method. The self-awareness that results from this letting go, being
undisturbed by conceptual thought, is totally uncontrived. You rest

in this state without thinking of anything. Since this is the king of samadhis, it generates an ascertainment consciousness. It is said that when [this ascertainment consciousness is generated], this is the true arising of the yoga of single-pointedness.[279] At this time you are relying on mindful effort that is intent on meditating. Therefore, while resting in this state, you cultivate the nature of that stillness without conceptual attachments. Whether there are mental fluctuations or not, by relaxing the mind into its natural state, you come to recognize the nature of mental movements while the mind remains still and at rest. Once you have achieved a natural state of stillness while the mind is fluctuating, the dividing line between stillness and mental fluctuation is erased. This is what it means to encounter the self-nature of the single-pointed state. That at this point one can experience mental stillness whether or not the mind fluctuates is something that has already been explained earlier.[280]

b. The yoga of nonelaboration

Then, by training in the clear and empty qualities of mind, you come to realize that all the phenomena of samsara and nirvana are emanations of your own mind, and having further concluded that the mind itself is unborn, all the phenomena of samsara and nirvana are purified into their natural state, which in turn vividly gives rise to the consciousness that directly ascertains the lack of elaborations, and one meditates. Since at this point the unerring yoga of the lack of elaborations has arisen, [406] this is called "doing away with the dividing line between error and liberation." When, in the wake of this, the appearances of the latent tendencies that grasp at signs occur, it is necessary to engage in a form of recollection called "automatic recollection of the primordial state," a recollection of the fact that whatever appears is by nature the primordial state of reality that arises as natural, unborn emptiness.

c. The yoga of the single taste

Eventually, even if mental appearances, the energy or effulgence of awareness, cause various conceptual fluctuations, there is no need to rely on other antidotes to block them; your continuous habituation to the reality that was already directly realized—that the mental conceptions themselves do not exist as true, permanent things, and that they are not generated by virtue of their own nature—gives rise to the recollection of the prior samadhi on reality. Whatever appears then arises strictly as the play of gnosis, and it becomes unnecessary to block appearances. Without needing to establish or prove that things are empty, the signs of subject-object dualism are naturally self-liberated. Once this occurs, all of the appearances of samsara, nirvana, and the three paths come to be known as the indivisible union of appearance and emptiness, and the unitary emptiness itself is understood to appear as the diversity of phenomena having various qualities. When this happens, you incorporate whatever appears into your meditation without allowing either [the side of appearances or of emptiness] to slip away. By so doing, the union of appearance and emptiness arises continuously within the mind, the dividing line between appearances and mind vanishes, and this leads to the generation within the mind of the yoga of the single taste.

d. The yoga of no-meditation
(A) The actual yoga of no-meditation

When you have meditated in this way, the true nature of mind—of mental conceptions, meditative experiences, and the wisdom of realizations—is directly perceived, and by the power of accustoming oneself to this insight, they vanish into the sphere of reality, and uncontrived, ordinary consciousness is recognized as reality. The vivid arising of the ascertainment consciousness purifies into the sphere of reality the aspects of the mind that involve recollection, intention, and exertion, and there then arises effortless true knowledge. Its nature is the gnosis of self-awareness.[281] Its quality is that everything manifests. Realization, the true nature of uncontrived reality, manifests; this is a realization that is devoid of mind in the sense that it transcends all dualistic aspects of the mind, notions like "the nature of uncontrived reality is what I am meditating on, and I am the meditator." Once this has occured, you are said to have generated in your mindstream the yoga of no-meditation.[282]

Compassion then manifests within the meditative equipoise. In the aftermath [or post-equipoise] state, there arises true knowledge that does not go beyond reality, and then, when the dividing line between equipoise and aftermath has been erased, you obtain the final fruit of meditation.

(B) As an aside, how to reconcile this system with the traditional explanation of the attainment of the stages of the path[283]

Although there are many incompatibilities between the method of practicing the four yogas, the five paths, and the ten stages (*bhumi*),[284] our own view is that the *yoga of single-pointed concentration* [407] corresponds to all of those "stages of devoted conduct" on or below the path of preparation.[285] As Lord Tsangpa Gyaré[286] states:

Single-pointedness is an experiential appearance.
It is a worldly path, and during it one accumulates karma.

Given that in this context [that is, in the context of single-pointed meditation] a confident ascertainment of the clarity and bliss of the mind does not arise in a nonconceptual manner, this state should not be confused with the experience of insight. There is a saying: "Single-pointedness is like being confined in a dark house." It is because single-pointed meditation covers the same ground again and again that Lord Milarepa states:

> What we desire is complete self-arisen realization.
> But if self-arisen realization does not arise,
> our wish should be not to lose analytical understanding.

It is through the wisdom that analyzes the view that you perfectly cut through reification while you are experiencing reality. Then, without cogitating in the way that the conceptual mind grasps at signs, you should meditate by settling the mind single-pointedly into the nature of the object. Lord Milarepa states:

> As soon as I meditate on Mahamudra,
> I settle single-pointedly into the nature of the object.
> I settle the mind by letting it go into a state of
>   nondistraction.

After that, you make manifest the gnosis that directly realizes the lack of elaborations. Hence, this is nothing but the path of seeing.

There are two explanations of what happens on or below the seventh bodhisattva stage.[287] In the general and pervasive tradition that uses the doctrinal terminology of the four yogas, the *yoga of the lack of elaborations* is considered to have both [a negative aspect or] "lack" and [a positive one or] "attainment"; and in this system it is necessary to accept that there occur forms of the aftermath consciousness—such as the carefree state and so forth—that are not embraced by equipoise. Hence, it is said to be correct to suggest a correspondence between [the yoga of nonelaboration] and all of the stages at or below the seventh. The *yoga of the single taste* corresponds to the eighth and ninth bodhisattva stages. The small and middling portions of the *yoga of no-meditation* correspond to the tenth stage, and the great stage of no-meditation corresponds to the state of buddhahood. And just as the yoga of no-meditation is divided into three parts, the other three yogas can also be divided into three—small, middling, and great—for a total of twelve.[288] There is also a nonmistaken exposition of the paths based on dividing each of those four yogas into six: those that see the true nature, those that do not, and so forth.

Moreover, if one were to reconcile this [system of the four yogas not with the exoteric stages of the bodhisattva path, just explained, but] solely with the [path system of] highest yoga tantra, it looks like this: having actualized the "analog clear light"[289] state within the "great" substage of the yoga of single-pointed concentration, through the yoga of nonelaborations, one enters into equipoise again and again on the "actual clear light." This causes one to actualize the "unified state of training." I see this explanation, given by the venerable Lhazig Repa,[290] to be correct, and so this is how [the correspondences to the highest yoga tantra] should be accepted.

Now we must discuss what Lord Sapen[291] has said in response to this in his *Distinguishing the Three Vows*: [408]

> Likewise, concerning single-pointedness and other
>   such states,

there would indeed be no contradiction if one could witness
   [that various sutras and tantras]
consider them to be paths [that belong to the stages of]
   devoted conduct.
But [the exponents of the four yogas] do not offer such an
   explanation.
And if these [stages of single-pointedness and so on] are
   considered the stages of noble beings (*aryas*),
it would contradict all of the sutras and tantras.[292]

At or below the state of single-pointedness, clarity in regard to
reality is only beginning to emerge. There is no direct perception
of reality at this point. Hence, one settles into single-pointedness
during the causal period, and one comes to possess a deep, single-
pointed experience of the nature of mind as the effect. Hence, giving
it such a name [for instance, the *yoga of single-pointedness*] is consistent
with the fact that on or below the path of preparation there is only
limited clarity in regard to the truth of reality, and that there are no
mental states during these early stages that directly perceive reality
in such a way that dualistic appearances have waned.[293] To claim
that all states between the first and seventh bodhisattva stages correspond to the "lack of elaborations" does *not* mean that there is no
lack of elaborations—no perception of reality—above that seventh
stage. Rather, "the lack of elaborations" is the name given to the
first of many instances of the realization of reality. Below this point,
from among the two, appearances and emptiness, it is necessary to
mostly rely on the thought [as opposed to the direct perception] of
emptiness *qua* lack of elaborations as an antidote to the grasping at
signs. That is why such a name ["yoga of the lack of elaborations"]

is used. This is also consistent with the fact that the texts of this tradition speak of the constant occurrence, on or below the seventh bodhisattva stage, of the actual manifestation of mental states in which there is grasping at true existence.

From the eighth stage and above, all dualities—for example, equipoise/aftermath and samsara/nirvana—are unified. Hence, the term *single taste* is used, for this is a state of union, a state in which appearance and emptiness have been unified into a single nature, which is the single taste. From that point on, even the antidotes that eliminate "what is to be abandoned" purify the obscurations naturally, and the gnosis that has unified the equipoise and aftermath states into a single nature has been actualized. This is what is called *no-meditation.*

Objection: Does this mean that there is nothing left to be purified by antidotes during the small and middling parts [of the yoga of no-meditation]?

Reply: [Those two lower stages] are called *no-meditation* indirectly—[i.e., by virtue of their analogy to that which truly bears] the name *great stage of no-meditation*—just as the goddess with the thin waistline is called "no-waist."[294] If such usage contradicts the sutras and tantras, then it is necessary for you to tell us why that other case—[the one in which the thin goddess is called "no-waist"]—is *not* contradictory.

Objection: It is incorrect to use this type of nomenclature, for there is no precedent for this in oral instructions.[295]

Reply: There are no serious religious polemicists who insist on offering explanations through conjoining terms to their etymologies. Hence, it is the fool who refuses to use language freely. If one argues that the simple use of nomenclature is incorrect because it is not known to others, then your own belief that each of the four initiations has its own view and philosophical stance would also be incorrect. And in particular, [409] a huge contradiction would ensue when you yourself claim that

> There is no difference in the way the view is explained
> in the Perfection of Wisdom and tantric scriptures.[296]

For having accepted that there is no difference in the way the view is explained in the sutras and tantras, you then go on to assert that each of the four empowerments of the highest yoga tantra has its own view. This is what the Lord Chennga Lhazig Repa states [in response to Sapen's critique of Mahamudra].

It does seem, however, that more research needs to be done concerning whether one of Lord Milarepa's songs does or does not state that something like the four yogas can occur during the path of ordinary beings.[297] Moreover, although the four yogas are clearly found within all of the scriptural and treasure texts of the ancient and new translation schools' Mahamudra literature, nonetheless, it is true that we do not see these explicitly taught in the authoritative Indian texts, but I think that the great masters of yore have resorted to this terminology in their oral instructions intending [to refer to their own experiences—to] what they have implicitly attained [in their own realizations].

In some Mahamudra explanations of later Karma, Drugpa, and Gampo Kagyü traditions,[298] one finds the claim that "the single-pointedness that belong to the mind of someone in the desire realm" and "the single-pointedness that belongs to the mind of someone who has attained calm abiding"—found in the instructions on

[Indian exoteric texts like] the *Stages of the Shravaka Path*,[299] the *Compendium of Metaphysics*,[300] the *Stages of Meditation*,[301] and the Perfection of Wisdom—are [what is meant by the Tibetan Mahamudra masters' term] *yoga of single-pointedness*; and that the term *lack of elaborations* [found in those same Indian exoteric texts is what is meant by the Tibetan Mahamudra masters' term] *yoga of the lack of elaborations*. But because it does not seem that these individuals are firm in their conviction, I will not elaborate on this theory in any detail here.

> This "day-maker" [the sun] of the oral tradition, which dispels the darkness of the three worlds,
> rising out of the "gods' path" [the sky], our investigations,
> is what causes the lotus of the correct view to blossom.
> Hence, it is a treasure banquet for the hordes of bees, the great meditators.

> Those who preach on the Great Seal and Great Perfection in the Land of Snows
> are mostly fools who, while deceiving others,
> preach methods of the Seal and Perfection different from the one just taught.
> Seeing that they have cast aside the fine path of scripture and reasoning, I have spoken up.

II. A little teaching on the interpretation of the Lord Tsongkhapa so as to sow seeds in regard to the profound view of reality

As the *Ornament of Realizations* states:

The altruistic mind of enlightenment is the desire to
attain
complete and perfect enlightenment for the sake of
others.³⁰²

What is it that disciples who have a propensity for the Mahayana
chiefly strive for? They strive for the unified state of the two bodies,
the Dharma body, which fulfills their own aim, and the form body,
which accomplishes the aims of others. What causes one to obtain
[this union of the two bodies]? The *Sixty Verses* states:

May these virtues I have created cause all beings
to perfect the accumulations of merit and gnosis [410]
and cause them to obtain the two holy bodies
that arise from merit and gnosis.³⁰³

*Knowledge of the path,*³⁰⁴ which amasses in a unified fashion the two
accumulations of merit and gnosis, depends on practicing the path
in such a way that method and wisdom are not separated one from
the other. Such a unified way of amassing the two accumulations
depends, first, on establishing the *view that is the ground,*³⁰⁵ and then
on gaining certainty in regard to the nonmistaken method of positing the two truths in a unified way. This is because the glorious
Chandrakirti³⁰⁶ has said:

The conventional truth is the method,
and the ultimate truth is what derives from that method
[i.e., it is the goal].

> Those who do not understand how to distinguish these
>   two truths
> follow false paths as the result of their misconceptions.[307]

By which one must implicitly understand that:

> Those who *properly* understand how to distinguish these
>   two truths
> are following a proper, nonmistaken path.[308]

This is what Chandrakirti means: yogis who have a propensity for the Mahayana and who fathom the two truths in a unified way strive to obtain the form body of a buddha as the result of their practice. To accomplish this form body, they must amass an extensive accumulation of merit, and to amass this they actively seek it with heartfelt devotion. This is because they have generated a profound certainty that the final, desired result arises through the amassing of the accumulation of merit as its cause. They generate such certainty because they have figured out how to lay the ground for certainty through the way they posit the conventional truth, the fact that things arise interdependently in such a way that specific causes give rise to specific results in a law-like way.

Such a yogi then enters into meditation on the view that unerringly realizes emptiness so as to obtain the result that is the Dharma body. Why? The resultant Dharma body is what arises from perfecting the practice of accustoming oneself to a cause that is generically similar to that Dharma body: the special accumulation of nonconceptual gnosis, the equipoise that realizes emptiness. The Dharma body does *not* arise from a cause that is generically *dis*similar to the

Dharma body. If one does not find certainty in regard to the fact that even conventionally no phenomenon has the slightest bit of existence by virtue of its own nature, even if one wishes to amass a proper accumulation of gnosis, one will not be able to do so. Therefore, in order to amass the accumulation of gnosis, it is necessary to ascertain emptiness in a nonmistaken way. To do that, it is necessary to ascertain that all phenomena are empty of intrinsic existence even at the conventional level. [411] Therefore, at the time of the *ground* it is necessary to have expertise in how the ultimate truth is posited.

To amass the accumulation of merit, it is necessary to find certainty concerning the fact that by practicing the vast aspects of *method*—charity and so on—the result, the attainment of a buddha's form body that acts for the sake of others, infallibly arises. It is also necessary to ascertain that even though cause and effect have not the slightest speck of intrinsic existence, the conventional world is nonetheless validly established: that so long as it is not analyzed or examined, one can posit the fact that everything functions simply by virtue of its imputation by name and thought. To accomplish that, it is necessary to have expertise in regard to how the conventional truth is posited, and hence, at the time of the ground, it is necessary to unerringly fathom how the two truths are established in a unified way. Then one ponders (a) how all cause and effect and all functionality can be correctly established as valid; (b) how there is nonetheless no such thing as an object's being established based on its own basis of designation; and how both [a and b] serve to reinforce one another until they have become one; one ponders this until empty interdependent arising appears as interdependent emptiness. Through such an understanding, the infallible relationship between cause and effect, which others—that is, the Madhyamikas' opponents—take as the reason for the impossibility of emptiness, becomes in our school the chief reason for the fact that emptiness is correct. By eliciting such certainty, every phenomenon becomes the basis for positing each of the two truths in a way that not only do they not contradict one another, they actually reinforce one another, each of the two truths serving to elicit certainty about the other. This is how one enters the path of amassing the two accumulations without any deficiencies and in a unified fashion.

Understanding that the doctrines of karma and its effects on the one hand and emptiness on the other are not contradictory is something that is exceedingly difficult to realize. Having seen how important such a realization is, the Buddha pretended to hesitate before agreeing to turn the wheel of the doctrine. As the *Precious Garland* states:

> Because this doctrine is so profound,
> fathoming how difficult it would be for beings to under-
>   stand it,
> the Conqueror Buddha
> initially turned away from teaching the doctrine.[309]

Those who have not awakened their mental abilities in regard to this profound point [that is, in regard to the compatibility of emptiness and causality] think that because phenomena are empty of essences even conventionally, they must be completely nonexistent. They thereby become nihilists in regard to the doctrine of causality. On the other hand, they think that because individual effects arise from their own causes, they must exist from the object's own side,

[412] which dooms them to believing that things exist by virtue of their own characteristics, and therefore dooms them to the belief that things exist intrinsically at the conventional level. This is to denigrate the doctrine of both truths. Hence, until such time as this faulty view is given up, there is no way to attain the mere liberation of an arhat, much less buddhahood. This is what the glorious Chandrakirti means when he states:

> For those who find themselves outside of the path of the
>   venerable master Nagarjuna,
> there is no way to obtain peace.
> They transgress the truth of conventional reality,
> and by transgressing it, they do not achieve emancipation.[310]

And Lord Maitripa states in his *Ten Verses on Reality*:

> Those who wish to understand reality
> should see it as neither possessing nor as lacking aspects.[311]

This is stating that those who wish to understand reality, the way things are, cannot do so based on the philosophy of the Sautrantika[312] school, which claims that things have aspects, nor based on the philosophy of the Vaibhashikas,[313] who believe that they have no aspects. And Lord Marpa[314] also states:

> Only fools claim that emptiness is nihilism.
> That claim is a nihilistic extreme that destroys the accumu-
>   lation of virtue.

And again he states:

> The Mind-Only school, the non-Buddhist Vaisheshikas,[315]
>   and so forth,
> each according to their own philosophical beliefs,
> are like those who believe that dead trees have flowers.

Request: Then please clearly articulate how, in the present context, one should set forth the two truths in a unified way.

Response: First of all, we accept that the object to be refuted—the self that, when refuted, we accept as bringing about the realization of no-self—is "existence by virtue of own-nature," or "intrinsic existence." As the *Commentary on the Four Hundred Stanzas* states:

> "Self" refers to an essence whose nature is such that it makes things independent of other things. The nonexistence of that self is "no-self." That self is understood in two ways, being divided according to whether it is a self of phenomena or of persons, and so there is a no-self of phenomena and a no-self of persons.[316]

And Buddhapalita[317] states:

> When he teaches that all phenomena have no self, the words "no-self" mean "no self-nature." This is because the word "self" is a technical term referring to "self-nature."[318]

It is necessary to identify such a self, the object to be refuted. For example, in order to ascertain that Devadatta does not exist at the site where Devadatta is not perceived by a valid cognition, it is necessary to know the Devadatta who does not exist. Likewise, to understand the meaning of "no-self" and "no essences" it is necessary to properly identify the self and essences that do not exist. [413] This is because unless the generic image of the object to be refuted appears to one, one does not ascertain the meaning of the no-self that is the refutation of that self. As the *Entering the Bodhisattva Practice* states:

> Without some sense of the thing being imagined,
> there is no apprehension of its unreality.[319]

We apprehend each and every person or phenomenon as a concrete thing, as existing from its own side, as existing in such a way that, rather than being merely posited by the internal mind, it is something that exists from its own side based on the object that is the basis of its imputation. That [false apprehension of the nature of objects] is how innate ignorance reifies things as intrinsically existing. That self-existence of phenomena that has been apprehended in this way by that innate ignorance is the "self that is to be refuted," or the "intrinsic existence" that, regardless of how unlikely it is, is to be identified. As the *Four Hundred Stanzas* states:

> None of these are independent,
> and therefore self-nature does not exist.[320]

And in the *Commentary* to this, Chandrakirti lists these [synonyms for self-nature]:

> Own-nature, essence, independence, not depending on
> something else...[321]

"Not depending on something else" does *not* mean "not depend-ing on causes and conditions." Rather, "something else" refers to the conventional consciousness that is the agent that perceives the object. Because things are not perceived as being posited by virtue of that consciousness, they are said to be perceived as "not depend-ing on something else." That is why the term "independence" is used; it refers to the special nature of objects, their own way of being. That is called the "nature that is the nonexistence of own-nature" and the "self-essence of things."

Therefore, rather than the object being conceived as posited by thought, there arises [in the mind a notion] that the object exists in its own right, [making it seem as though it exists] by virtue of its own nature; this is the "self that is to be refuted." The refuta-tion of that self is not a refutation that leaves one bereft of action. Rather, witnessing that there is a conceptual thought that conceives of the object to be refuted as existing in that false way, and that this is what binds sentient beings to samsara against their will, one sets out to eliminate that ignorance by destroying the object of that misconception. This is because the ignorance that binds sentient beings to samsara is innate ignorance.

How then does one go about refuting the object to be refuted? Suppose that you mistake a striped rope for a snake and that it frightens you. [To dispel the fear that there is a snake] you must correct that error by determining that there is no snake as apprehended by the mind. There is nothing else you can do, no other way [to rid yourself of the fear]. Likewise, [in order to get rid of ignorance] [414] you have to use correct reasons to ascertain that the object of the innate grasping at true existence—a grasping that apprehends things as if they existed from their own side—does not exist, and you then have to accustom yourself to that fact. The nonexistence of the object as it is apprehended by the innate ignorance that grasps at true existence cannot be established simply by fiat. Rather, it must be *proven* using a stainless collection of scriptures and reasoning. What is more, you must base this proof on a prior analysis that uses analytical wisdom, and you must not understand this reality as something other than the object's lack of true existence. Simply entertaining no thoughts whatsoever is not allowed. As the last of the *Stages of Meditation* states:

> Therefore, you should see that the states of no-thought and no-cogitation found in the holy Dharma have correct analytical knowledge as a prerequisite. This is because the states of no-thought and no-cogitation can only be brought about by correct analytical knowledge and in no other way.[322]

And the second of the *Stages of Meditation* states:

> So wisdom analyzes things in this way, and when yogis no longer cling to the nature of things as ultimately real, they then enter into a nonconceptual samadhi [on that truth]. They also realize the lack of self-nature of *all*

phenomena. But whoever does not meditate using wisdom to analyze the nature of things, whoever meditates only so as to abandon cogitation, never gets rid of the misconceptions of ignorance, never realizes the lack of own-nature. Why? Because this form of meditation lacks the light of wisdom.[323]

Therefore, even though the reasoning that analyzes reality finds no phenomenon whatsoever at the culmination of that analysis, one is led to certainty concerning the fact that in a merely nominal way, at the level of conventions, where one does *not* engage in analysis or examination of this type, all of the functionality of the world—such as the fact that effects arise from their causes and so on—can be posited as validly established. This is what Tsongkhapa accepts as "training in amassing the two accumulations in a unified way." It is what Tsongkhapa has in mind when he states in his *Great Exposition of the Stages of the Path*:

> The stainless system of those Indian sages
> shows how it is possible for things that lack intrinsic existence, which are like illusions—
> samsara and nirvana, interdependent arising—can function.
> I have given a brief explanation of this in a way that is easy to understand.
> You, my friends, who train in the texts of the profound Middle Way,
> no matter how difficult it may be for you to reconcile in your own minds
> the interdependence of a causality that lacks intrinsic existence, [415]

such is the system of the Middle Way.

What a thing of beauty to rely on the method that advocates
      such an approach to reality.[324]

Let us practice in accordance with these words.

✳   ✳   ✳

In order to reach the state of buddhahood,
three methods of practicing the essence
of the resultant vajra vehicle of the tantras
and of the causal vehicle of the perfections have been taught:
the view of the Great Middle Way,
that of the Great Seal, and that of the Great Perfection.
These were well known among the translators and pandits
      of yore.
But then King Trisong Detsen
decreed the highest yoga tantra to be a concealed doctrine,
which slightly impeded—because it changed—the well-known
      oral tradition.
As a result, in the eyes of the three schools that came afterward,[325]
      the ancient translations
were claimed "not to be translations of Indian texts," and became
      an object of polemic.
Although there are both authentic and a few inauthentic texts
among the scriptures and treasures of the Great Seal and Great
      Perfection,
here I have chosen to harmonize the views
of the awareness-holder Padmasambhava and Vimalamitra,[326]

of the many scholar-practitioners who were their followers,

of Dampa Sangyé, Marpa, and Milarepa,

of Dagpo Lhajé, the father, and his spiritual sons.

This ecumenical method of teaching disciples

was taught to various fortunate individuals

by the holy emanation Sanggyé Tsöndrü.[327]

using true scriptures and stainless reasoning.

I have now completed this *Wish-Fulfilling Jewel of the Oral Tradition*.

May the act of writing this work cause beings to quickly obtain

the state of the three bodies.

Colophon

The composition of the *Wish-Fulfilling Jewel of the Oral Tradition*, a clarification of how the general and specific points of the practice of the path can be identified in a general view that pervades all the traditions, was requested over and over again by the master of ten treatises who hails from Dotö, Rinchen Özer, by the emanation Trinlé Lhündrub,[328] and by others. It is based on the many instructions of the Ancient and New Schools I so kindly received from the lord of yogis, Nyida Sanggyé,[329] instructions on such topics as the Middle Way, Mahamudra, Dzogchen, the Pacifier (Zhiché), the Practice of Severance (Chöyül), the six-limbed yoga of the Kalachakra (Jordrug),[330] and the six Dharmas of Naropa (Chödrug).[331] It is also based on having been later nourished by the nectar of the teachings of the lord of scholars, Peljor Sönam Lhündrub,[332] and others.

It was composed in the bird year [1609] at the abbatial seat of the Jé College of Sera Monastery by the Khön monk [Peljor Lhündrub], an individual who, without sectarian bias, is engaged in hearing, thinking, and contemplating the precious sutra and tantra teachings of the Land of Snows.

May goodness prevail.

The scribe was the emanation Trinlé Lhündrub.

Appendix 1

The Works of Khöntön Peljor Lhündrub Mentioned in the Fifth Dalai Lama's Biography

Some thirty-three works of Khöntön Peljor Lhündrub are mentioned in the Fifth Dalai Lama's *Record of Teachings Received* (*Thob yig*).[333] What follows is a list of Khöntön Rinpoché's works mentioned in other sources, chiefly the Fifth Dalai Lama's biography of his master, *A Chariot of Faith for the Fortunate*.[334] While most of the works mentioned in the Fifth Dalai Lama's *Chariot* are also found in his *Record*, a few are not. Some of the wording in the titles also differs in the two lists. Since most of the works mentioned here are no longer available, I have added a column ("Date") to denote at what point in the *Chariot* narrative the Dalai Lama mentions various texts. Needless to say, this gives us at most a rough idea of when various works might have been penned, and should not be considered definitive, unless, of course, a specific date of composition is mentioned or known from other sources. I have also noted, in the list that follows, when a work is mentioned in Akhu Rinpoché's list of rare works; the reference is to Dr. Lokesh Chandra, *Materials for a History of Tibetan Literature* (MHTL) (Kyoto: Rinsen Book Co., 1981).

Date	Tibetan Title	English Title	Reference in "Chariot" etc.
1583	དབུ་མ་ལྟ་ཁྲིད།	A teaching on the Middle Way view	*Shing rta*, fol. 12a; *Gu bkra*, p. 300; MHTL 11465
1583	དཀོན་མཆོག་གསུམ་ལ་ སྐྱབས་སུ་འགྲོ་ཚུལ་གྱི་ གདམས་པ་ཟབ་མོ་སྙན་ བརྒྱུད་ཁྱད་པར་གསུམ་ ལྡན། [335]	Profound instructions on going for refuge to the Three Jewels: an oral tradition with three special features	*Shing rta*, fol. 12a; MHTL 11219
After 1605; or in 1614 [336]	བསྟན་རྩིས།	A timeline	*Shing rta*, fol. 25a
After 1605	འཕྲུལ་སྣང་གཙུག་ལག་ཁང་ གི་དཀར་ཆག	An inventory of the Trülnang Temple (i.e., the Jokhang Temple in Lhasa)	*Shing rta*, fol. 25a
After 1605	གསང་འདུས་སྨོན་ལམ།	A prayer to Guhyasamāja	*Shing rta*, fol. 25a
After 1605	ས་གསུམ་མ།	The three worlds (a prayer)	*Shing rta*, fol. 25a
After 1605	ཇ་མཆོད་ཀྱི་ཊཱི་ཀ།	A commentary on the tea offering	*Shing rta*, fol. 25a
After 1605	རབ་གནས་ཀྱི་དོགས་དཔྱོད།	Clarifications on the consecration [ritual]	*Shing rta*, fol. 25a
1609 [337]	ལྟ་བ་སྤྱི་ཁྱབ།	The general and pervasive view	*Shing rta*, fol. 31a; *Gu bkra*, p. 300; MHTL 11466
Around 1627	དཔལ་རྡོ་རྗེ་འཇིགས་བྱེད་ཀྱི་ འཕྲིན་ལས་བཞིའི་སྦྱིན་སྲེག་ བྱེད་ཚུལ།	How to perform a Vajrabhairava burnt offering ritual for the four purposes	*Shing rta*, fol. 35b

Around 1627	སྨན་བླ་བདེ་གཤེགས་བདུན་གྱི་དབང་ཆོག་ཕན་བདེའི་འབྱུང་གནས།	The empowerment ritual of the seven tathāgatas of the Medicine Buddha [pantheon]: the source of benefit and happiness	*Shing rta*, fol. 35b
Around 1627	ཐམས་ཅད་མཁྱེན་པ་དགེ་འདུན་རྒྱ་མཚོའི་བླ་མ་མཆོད་པའི་རྣམ་བཤད།	An explanation of the "Offering to the Spiritual Master" by the omniscient Gendün Gyatso	*Shing rta*, fol. 35b
Around 1627	བྱང་གཏེར་ཐུགས་སྒྲུབ་ཀྱི་མངོན་རྟོགས་གསར་མ་ལྟར་ཕྱག་འདོན།	The chanted ritual of the "Mental Accomplishment Realization" of the Northern Treasures according to the New schools	*Shing rta*, fol. 35b
Around 1627	སྒྲུབ་ཐབས་རྡོས་གྲུབ་རྒྱ་མཚོ་བུམ་བཀྱེད།	The vase ritual of the "Ocean of Sādhana Accomplishments"	*Shing rta*, fol. 35b
Around 1627	རྒྱལ་བ་ཙོང་ཁ་པར་འཇམ་དཔལ་ཞལ་གཟིགས་ཆུལ་བརྫས་བཅིངས་པའི་འགྲོ་ལ་(འགྲེལ་པ?)སློ་བཟང་དགོངས་རྒྱན།	The intention of Lozang: an interpretation of the symbols involved in Tsongkhapa's visions of Mañjuśrī	*Shing rta*, fol. 35b
Around 1627	ཐྲེས་ཀྱི་ཕུར་པའི་ལོ་རྒྱས།	A history of the ritual dagger of Jé [College]	*Shing rta*, fol. 35b
Around 1627[338]	བདེ་བ་ཅན་སྨོན་ལམ་གྱི་འགྲེལ་པ།	A commentary on the "Sukhavatī Prayer"	*Shing rta*, fol. 35b

Around 1627	བསྐུན་བཅོད་མངོན་རྟོགས་ རྒྱན་རྩ་འགྲེལ་གྱི་ཊིཀྐ་ཤིན་ ཏུ་རྒྱས་པ།	An extremely detailed commentary on the *Ornament of Realizations* root text and its commentary	*Shing rta*, fol. 35b
Around 1627	གསོལ་འདེབས་སྨོན་ལམ་ ཞལ་གདམས་དྲི་ལམ།	[Various] petitionary and other prayers, advice, and responses to questions	*Shing rta*, fol. 35b
1628[339]	འཇིགས་བྱེད་ཀྱི་ཆོས་འབྱུང་ ནོར་བུའི་ཕྲེང་བ།	A garland of jewels: a history of the Yamāntaka [lineage]	*Shing rta*, fol. 35a–b
1628	མ་འོངས་འབྱུང་འགྱུར་གྱི་ རིམ་པ་བཤད་པའི་ལུང་ བསྟན་ལྔ་པ།[340]	Five [verses] of prophecy that ex-plain the sequence of what will happen in the future	*Shing rta*, fol. 36b
1628	ཡངས་པའི་རྒྱལ་ཁམས་བདེ་ ཐབས་ཀྱི་སྐུ་རིམ་པ་ཐན་བདེ་ འབྱུང་གནས།	A source of hap-piness: systematic exhortations to prac-tice; rituals to bring about the happiness of the country as a whole	*Shing rta*, fol. 35b

Appendix 2

THE INCARNATION LINEAGE OF KHÖNTÖN RINPOCHÉ

THIS LIST is based on several sources: (1) the incarnations of the Changkya Lamas (Lcang skya bla ma) found in a work of Longdöl Lama (Klong rdol bla ma), *Rgya bod du byon pa'i bstan 'dzin*, fol. 399a; (2) E. Gene Smith, *Among Tibetan Texts: History and Literature of the Himalayan Plateau* (Boston: Wisdom Publications, 2001), p. 146, (3) Michael Henss, "Rölpai Dorje—Teacher of the Empire" (http://www.asianartgallery.co.uk/research/current.php). A list of the former lives of Khönton Rinpoché is also found in *Shing rta*, fol. 3a ff.; and in a work by Könchog Jigmé Wangpo (Dkon mchog 'jigs med dbang po), *Rje btsun thams cad mkhyen pa lcang skya rol pa'i rdo rje'i 'khrung rabs kyi phreng ba gtam du brjod pa ngo mtshar dad pa'i ljong shing*, in *The Collected Works of Dkon-mchog 'jigs-med dbang-po*, Gaden Sungrab Mi-nyam Gyunphel Series 22 (New Delhi: Ngawang Gelek Demo, 1971), vol. 2. See also Tashi Densapa, "A Short Biography of 'Gro-mgon Chos-rgyal 'Phags-pa," *Bulletin of Tibetology*, New Series, 3 (1977): 7–14. As an aside, the Eighth Zhamarpa (Zhwa dmar Dpal chen Chos kyi don grub, 1695–1732) mentions that he believed that Lha bzang khan's candidate for the reincarnation of the Sixth Dalai Lama was in actuality a reincarnation of Khönton Rinpoché.[341]

1. Buddha Amitābha (Sangs rgyas Snang ba mtha' yas). This is not found in *Shing rta*.

2. Arhat Chunda (Dgra bcom pa Tsunda). He was a disciple of Śākyamuni.

3. Śākyamitra (Shākya bshes gnyen). He was a disciple of Nāgārjuna and a lineage holder of the latter's Guhyasamāja teachings.

4. Darpaṇa Ācārya (Darban ātsarya). He is identified as an Indian Yamāntaka yogi, but he is not mentioned in *Shing rta*, nor is he found in Khöntön Rinpoché's own *History of the Yamāntaka Lineage*.

5. Kawa Peltseg (Ska ba dpal brtsegs, eighth century). He was one of the great Tibetan translators of the early dissemination period.

6. The great Nyingma adept Dropugpa (Gsang sngags rnying ma'i grub chen Sgro phug pa, b. eleventh century). Khöntön Rinpoché states that Zur Datsa Horpo (Zur mda' tsha hor po, 1074–1134) "is probably the Lord Dropugpa"; *Bzhin rje gshed chos 'byung*, pp. 49–50.

7. Chenrizig Wang Sisiripa (Spyan ras gzigs dbang Si si ri pa). E. Gene Smith and Michael Henss identify this figure as Se ston ri pa (d. 1233), but the dates of this figure do not fit with the present scheme. *Shing rta*, fol. 3b, states that he hailed from the region of É and was an accomplished Avalokiteśvara yogi.

8. Kadampa Geshe Langri Tangpa (Bka' gdams pa Glang ri thang pa Rdo rje seng ge, 1054–1123). He is not mentioned in *Shing rta*, nor do his dates fit into the present scheme. But Langri Tangpa is found in the list of Könchog Jigmé Wangpo.

9. Sakyapa Lodrö Gyeltsen (Sa skya pa Blo gros rgyal mtshan,

1235–80); in other words, Chögyel Pagpa (Chos rgyal 'phags pa). He was the nephew of Sakya Pandita, the teacher to Kublai Khan, and the first viceroy of Tibet under the Mongols.

10. Lama Dampa Sönam Gyeltsen (Bla ma dam pa Bsod nams rgyal mtshan, 1312–75). Here I follow *Shing rta*, fol. 4a, where we find the next incarnation after Pagpa to be Drogön Sönampa ('Gro mgon Bsod nams pa, also called Bla ma bdag nyid chen po Bzang po dpal). Longdöl Lama lists here Sa skya pa 'gro mgon Chos rgyal 'phags pa (Chögyel Pagpa, 1235–80), clearly a duplication of the previous entry.

11. Jamchen Chöjé Shakya Yeshé (Byams chen chos rje Shākya ye shes, 1354–1435). He was a disciple of Tsongkhapa and the founder of Sera Monastery. On Khöntönpa's recognition as the reincarnation of this master, see *Shing rta*, fol. 26a. It should be noted, however, that Jamchen Chöjé was born twenty-one years before the death of the previous incarnation in this list, Lama Dampa.

12. Sera Jetsün Chökyi Gyeltsen (Se ra rje btsun Chos kyi rgyal mtsan, 1469–1544). He composed the textbooks (*yig cha*) of the Jé College of Sera.

13. **Khöntön Peljor** ('Khon ston dpal 'byor, 1561–1637).

14. Khedrub Dragpa Özer (Mkhas grub [or Lcang skya] Grags pa 'od zer, d. 1641). Although the date of his birth is not known, this master, who made Gönlung Jampa Ling Monastery (Dgon lung byams pa gling) his seat, lived a long life. He must therefore have been born substantially before Khöntön Rinpoché died. Dragpa Özer served as abbot of Gönlung from 1630 to 1633.[342]

15. Changkya Ngagwang Lozang Chöden (Lcang skya ngag dbang

blo bzang chos ldan, 1642–1714), the first[343] Changkya incarnation). He served as abbot of Gönlung from 1688 to 1690.[344]

16. Changkya Yeshé Tenpai Drönmé (Lcang skya Ye shes bstan pa'i sgron me, 1717–86), also known as Changkya Rölpai Dorjé (Lcang skya Rol pa'i rdo rje, the second Changkya incarnation). One of the greatest scholars of the Gelug school, he served as abbot of Gönlung from 1763/64 to 1769/70.[345]

17. Changkya Yeshé Tenpai Gyeltsen (Lcang skya Ye shes bstan pa'i rgyal mtshan, 1787–1846), the third Changkya Rinpoché.

18. Changkya Yeshé Tenpai Nyima (Lcang skya Ye shes bstan pa'i nyi ma, 1849–59/75),[346] the fourth Changkya lama.

19. Changkya Lozang Yeshé Tenpai Gyatso (Lcang skya Blo bzang ye shes bstan pa'i rgya mtsho, 1860/78–1870/88), the fifth Changkya incarnation.

20. Changkya Lozang Pelden Tenpai Drönmé (Lcang skya Blo bzang dpal ldan bstan pa'i sgron me, b. circa 1871 or 1890/91), the sixth Changkya Rinpoché.

21. Changkya Chöying Yeshé Dorjé (Lcang skya Chos dbyings ye shes rdo rje, 1891–1957/58), the seventh Changkya incarnation. He apparently died in Taiwan.[347]

22. Changkya Dönyo Gyatso (Lcang skya don yod rgya mtsho, b. circa 1980), the eighth Changkya incarnation. He was identified at age eighteen by His Holiness the Dalai Lama, who ordained him in 2004. He presently studies at the Gomang College of Drepung Monastery in India.

Notes

1 'Khon ston Dpal 'byor lhun grub. This account of Khöntön Rinpoché's life is based chiefly on the earliest biography, written by his student the Fifth Dalai Lama, the *Khyab bdag 'khor lo'i dbang phyug dpal 'byor lhun grub kyi rnam thar skal bzang dad pa'i shing rta*, found in the Fifth Dalai Lama's Gsung 'bum (Collected Works), vol. *nya*, pp. 609–96 (hereafter *Shing rta*); the text was written in 1645, eight years after Khöntön Rinpoché's death. I have also consulted the entry for 'Khon ston Dpal 'byor lhun grub in Yongs 'dzin Ye shes rgyal mtshan (1713–93), *Lam rim bla ma brgyud pa'i rnam thar* (Lhasa: Bod ljongs mi dmangs dpe skrun khang, 1990), pp. 794–96 (hereafter *Bla brgyud*), which relies, as do most of the other biographies, on the Fifth Dalai Lama's work. The earliest Nyingma biography of Khöntön Rinpoché known to me is found in the *Guru bkra shis chos 'byung*; Gu ru Bkra shis ngag dbang blo gros, *Gu bkra'i chos 'byung* (Mtsho sngon: Krung go'i bod kyi shes rig dpe skrung khang, 1990), pp. 299–300, hereafter *Gu bkra*. This work was written between 1807 and 1813. Guru Trashi's text appears to be the chief source for Dudjom Rinpoché's biography, found in Bdud 'joms 'Jigs bral ye shes rdo rje, *Gangs jongs rgyal bstan yongs rdzogs kyi phyi mo snga 'gyur rdo rje theg pa'i bstan pa rin po che ji ltar byung ba'i tshul dag cing gsal bar brjod pa lha dbang g.yul las rgyal ba'i rnga bo che'i sgra dbyangs* (Bound book; no bibliographical information other than the date, 1990), pp. 336–39, hereafter *Bdud 'joms*; translated in *The Nyingma School of Tibetan Buddhism* (Boston: Wisdom Publications, 2002), vol. 1, pp. 677–78. A short modern biography of Khöntönpa is to be found in Sgo mang Ngag dbang lung rtogs' foreword to Khöntönpa's *History of the Yamāntaka Lineage*, the *'Jam dpal gzhin rje gshed skor gyi bla ma brgyud pa'i chos 'byung gdul bya'i re 'dod skong ba yid bzhin nor bu'i phreng ba*, hereafter *Gzhin rje gshed chos 'byung* (Dharamsala: Library of Tibetan Works and Archives, 2005). A brief mention of Khöntönpa is found in Ko shul Grags pa 'byung gnas and Rgyal ba Blo bzang mkhas grub, *Gangs can mkhas grub rim byon ming mdzod* [hereafter *Ming mdzod*] (Chengdu: Kan

su'u mi rigs dpe skrun khang, 1992), pp. 235–37; and in Bstan 'dzin lung rtogs nyi ma's *Rdozgs chen chos byung chen mo* (Beijing: Krung go'i bod rig pa dpe skrun khang, 2004), pp. 167–68. For references to Khöntön Rinpoché in other Tibetan works, see Dan Martin, in collaboration with Yael Bentor, *Tibetan Histories: A Bibliography of Tibetan-Language Historical Works* (London: Serindia, 1997), entry 196, p. 99. Khöntön Rinpoché is also briefly mentioned as the teacher of G.yul rgyal nor bu (1550?–1607) in Per Sørensen and Guntram Hazod, with Tsering Gyalbo, *Rulers of the Celestial Plain: Ecclesiastical and Secular Hegemony in Medieval Tibet, a Study of Tshal Gung-thang* (Vienna: Verlag des Österreichischen Akademie der Wissenschaften, 2007), vol. II, pp. 245 and 768n10.

2   'Khon. *Bla brgyud*, p. 795, calls this the Mañjuśrī Khön lineage ('Jam dbyangs 'khon gyi rigs). The Fifth Dalai Lama gives a long explanation of the Khön clan's history in *Shing rta*, fol. 5a–b. Elsewhere in the work, he explains the clan's connections to the deity Mañjuśrī.

3   Skyong gar.

4   In Klong rdol bla ma's *Rgya bod du byon pa'i bstan 'dzin gyi skyes bu dam pa rnams kyi mtshan tho*, Asian Classics Input Project (ACIP) digital text, ref. no. S6552E_T, fol. 385a, he is called E pa Dpal 'byor lhun grub. The Fifth Dalai Lama explains that the region where Khöntön Rinpoché was born is called É because it has the shape of the Tibetan letter "e"; *Shing rta*, fol. 6b.

5   Tshe dbang nor rgyas. All of the old sources give Tsewang Norgyé as the father's name. *Ming mdzod*'s "Tsewang Norbu" is therefore almost certainly an error. *Gu bkra*, pp. 299–300, traces the lineage of the *Guhyabargbha* from the Fourth Zhamar (Zhwa dmar Chos grags ye shes, 1453–1524) to the eighteenth abbot of Drigung ('Bri gung Rin chen phun tshogs, 1509–57) to Nyida Sanggyé (see below) to Khöntön Rinpoché's father.

6   The *Magical Net* or *Secret Nucleus* (*Guhyagarbha*) *Tantra* is the chief tantra of the *mahā yoga* division of the nine vehicles of the Nyingma tradition that His Holiness mentions in his lecture. See Gyurme Dorje, "The *Guhyagarbhatattvaviniścayamahātantra* and Its XIVth Century Tibetan Commentary: Phyogs bcu mun sel" (Ph.D. dissertation, University of London, 1987).

7   *Gu bkra*, p. 299, and *Bdud 'joms*, pp. 336–37, also state that he received from Nyida Sanggyé (Nyi zla sangs rgyas, fifteenth–sixteenth centuries) various other Nyingma teachings, including the lineage of the "Seminal Essence of the Clear Expanse" (*Klong gsal snying thig*), an important Dzogchen tradition revealed by Ratna Lingpa (Ratna gling pa, 1403–79). And in fact, among the works of Khöntön Rinpoché mentioned by the Fifth Dalai Lama, we find an

Homage to the Lineage of the Dzogchen Seminal Essence of the Clear Expanse (*Rdzogs pa chen po klong gsal snying thig gi brgyud 'debs*), a work that is unfortunately no longer extant.

8 Se ra byes drwa tshang.

9 Sgro phug pa. See *Gu bkra*, p. 299, and *Bdud 'joms*, p. 337. This important master, the son of the great Zurchungpa (Zur chung pa), belonged to the late eleventh and early twelfth centuries. *Gu bkra*, pp. 274–314, gives a fairly lengthy biography of Dropugpa. Both Dropugpa and Khöntön Rinpoché are also found in the incarnation lineage of the famous Gelug master Changkya Rolpai Dorjé (Lcang skya Rol pa'i rdo rje, 1717–86); see Klong rdol bla ma, *Rgya bod du byon pa'i bstan 'dzin*, fol. 399a, and appendix 2.

10 *Gsar rnying rim med*. This is how he is known in his biographies and also by later scholars like Sumpa Khenpo (Sum pa mkhan po Ye shes dpal 'byor, 1704–88). See *Tibetan Chronological Tables of Jam-dbyaṅs bźad-pa and Sumpa mkhan-po*, trans. by Alaka Chattopadhyaya and Sanjit Kumar Sadhukhan (Sarnath: Central Institute of Higher Tibetan Studies, 1993), p. 197.

11 Rgyal mo 'dzom.

12 *Blo sbyong*. On this genre of Tibetan literature, see Thupten Jinpa, trans., *Mind Training: The Great Collection* (Boston: Wisdom Publications, 2006); and Michael J. Sweet, "Mental Purification (Blo sbyong): A Native Tibetan Genre of Religious Literature," in José I. Cabezón and Roger R. Jackson, eds., *Tibetan Literature: Studies in Genre* (Ithaca, NY: Snow Lion Publications, 1996), pp. 244–60.

13 *Shing rta*, fol. 7b.

14 Bsod nams rgya mtsho, 1543–88. See Martin Brauen, *The Dalai Lamas: A Visual History* (Chicago: Serindia, 2005), pp. 53–59.

15 The vows of a Buddhist lay person consist of not lying, not killing, not stealing, not engaging in sexual misconduct, and not drinking alcohol. *Gu bkra*, p. 299, and *Bdud 'joms*, p. 336 (Dudjom Rinpoché, *The Nyingma School*, p. 677), state that Khöntön Rinpoché was ordained (*rab tu byung*) by the Third Dalai Lama at this point in his life—that is, at the age of ten.

16 Bsod nams rnam rgyal.

17 *Shing rta*, fol. 9a. The Fifth Dalai Lama = Rgyal ba Ngag bang blo bzang rgya mtsho (1617–82). Samten Karmay, *Secret Visions of the Fifth Dalai Lama* (London: Serindia, 1999), p. 3, states that Khöntön Rinpoché first met the Fifth Dalai Lama when the latter was nineteen years of age, and that it was Khöntön Rinpoché who was responsible for initiating the Fifth Dalai Lama into Dzogchen and other Nyingma teachings. If this is true, it means that

although Peljor Lhündrub only served as the Dalai Lama's tutor for two years, he would have a profound influence on his student, spurring in him an interest in the tantric teachings of the Nyingma school that would last throughout the Fifth Dalai Lama's life.

18   This "ordination" may be a reference to what has come to be known as *bar ma rab byung*, a level of ordination between lay and novice, since we know from the Dalai Lama's biography that Khöntön Rinpoché did not receive formal novice vows until later in his life.

19   *Mchod gnas.*

20   See Zahiruddin Ahmad, *Sino-Tibetan Relations in the Seventeenth Century* (Rome: IsMEO, 1970), pp. 1578ff.

21   Dwags po grwa tshang, a teaching institution in southeastern Tibet founded by a student of Tsongkhapa, Jé Lodrö Tenpa (Rje Blo gros bstan pa) or Lodrö Gyatso (Blo gros rgya mtsho) in 1473. Khöntönpa, however, states in his *Gzhin rje gshed chos 'byung*, p. 131, that it was Jetsün Sherab Senggé (Rje Shes rab seng ge, 1383–1445), founder of Gyümé, who "founded the Mthong smon grwa tshang at Gsang phu, which today is known as Dwags po grwa tshang"; *gsang phur mthong smon grwa tshang btsugs pa da lta dwags po grwa tshang du grags pa 'di yin.* This may be an error. See Sde srid sangs rgyas rgya mtsho, *Dga' ldan chos 'byung bai ḍurya ser po* (Mtsho sngon: Mi rigs dpe skrung khang 1991), pp. 197–98. Klong rdol bla ma, *Rgya bod du byon pa'i bstan 'dzin*, fol. 388b, lists Khöntön Rinpoché as one of the great scholars who hailed from Dagpo College. On the date of his first visit to Dagpo, I follow *Shing rta*, fol. 8a, rather than *Ming mdzod*, which claims that he entered the college at age ten.

22   *Shing rta*, fol. 8a: *dags po grwa tshang gi slob dpon skal bzang rgya mtsho.* Desi Sanggyé Gyatso (Sde srid, *Baiḍurya ser po*, p. 197) lists this figure as one of the abbots of the monastery, who held the abbacy between Epa Gendün Lhündrub (E pa Dge 'dun lhun grub) and Ei Teurapa Gendün Samdrub (E'i te'u ra pa Dge 'dun bsam grub). Desi also lists the textbooks used at the college and states that in his day there were three hundred monks studying there.

23   Nyi zla sangs rgyas (b. fifteenth/sixteenth century), a lineage master in the Northern Treasures (Byang gter) tradition and, as mentioned earlier, one of the major lineage figures in the transmission of the *Magical Net Tantra* of the Nyingma school. He was a student of Drigung Zurpa Rinchen Püntsog ('Bri gung zur pa Rin chen phun tshogs, 1509–57), also known as Natsog Rangdröl (Sna tshogs rang grol). See Dudjom Rinpoche, *The Nyingma School*, vol. 1, pp. 676–77.

24   For a list of these teachings, see *Shing rta*, fols. 9b–10a.

25   'Ol kha Blo bzang rgya mtsho. Sumpa Khenpo (*Tibetan Chronological Tables*, p. 205) states that Khöntön Rinpoché entered Dagpo College in 1580.

26   *Bla brgyud*, p. 794, states that he completed all of his studies of the five classical subjects—Perfection of Wisdom, Middle Way Philosophy, Monastic Discipline, Metaphysics, and Logic—at Dagpo; but the earlier *Shing rta*, fol. 11b, chiefly mentions three subjects: Perfection of Wisdom (*phar phyin*), Middle Way (*dbu ma*), and Logic (*tshad ma*). It does later mention his study of Monastic Discipline and Metaphysics ('*dul mdzod*) at Dagpo, fol. 12a, but only in passing. Since Khöntön Rinpoché did not receive full ordination until much later in his life, it would be a bit unusual (though not impossible) that he would have studied Vinaya at this point.

27   *Dbu ma lta khrid*. This text is no longer available, but the Fifth Dalai Lama's *Shing rta*, fol. 12a, informs us that this is when the work was written.

28   E Ri sgo chos sde, founded by Tsangpa Ngagwang Trashi (Gtsang pa Ngag dbang bkra shis). See Sde srid, *Baiḍurya ser po*, p. 204.

29   Se ra byes grwa tshang. This is one of three colleges of Sera Monastery. The Jé College was founded by Kunkyenpa (Kun mkhyen Blo gros rin chen seng ge, b. fifteenth century).

30   Byams chen chos rje Shākya ye shes (1354–1435). Jamchen Chöjé founded Sera in 1419.

31   Se ra rje btsun Chos kyi rgyal mtshan (1469–1544). On the life of this important figure, see Elijah Sacvan Ary, "Logic, Lives and Lineage: Jetsun Chökyi Gyaltsen's Ascension and the *Secret Biography of Khedrup Geleg Pelzang*" (Ph.D. dissertation, Harvard University, 2007), chap. 3.

32   Dpal 'byor bsod nams lhun grub (b. 1553). Peljor Sönam Lhündrub is an interesting figure in his own right. Born into the Nyingma Zur clan, he too was an important figure in the Northern Treasures lineage. He served as abbot of Sera's Jé College before Trinlé Lhündrub; see the following note.

33   'Phrin las lhun grub (b. sixteenth century). This figure, who hailed from Dragkar (Brag dkar), preceded Khöntön Rinpoché as abbot of Jé College.

34   *Gling bsre*, one of the degrees of geshé (*dge bshes*), a kind of doctorate in exoteric Buddhist doctrinal studies. *Shing rta*, fol. 13a: '*gyangs med du gling bs[r]e grub*. *Bla bryud*, p. 795, only mentions that he did the monastic rounds and does not mention any degree.

35   Rtses/rtsed thang. *Shing rta*, fol. 13b.

36   *Rab 'byams pa*: higher than the *lingsé*, in this degree the candidate must show extraordinary knowledge of a wide variety of texts. It is interesting to note

that the degree was not awarded by his home monastery of Sera. Candidates for the Rabjampa degree had to submit to examinations outside their home institution to receive this degree.

37 Skyid shod.

38 Dga' ldan chos rje Byams pa rgya mtsho (1516–90), the twenty-fourth holder of the Ganden throne.

39 Lhas ltag dgon.

40 Spyan snga Chos dpal bzang po (b. sixteenth century).

41 *Lam rim chen mo*; see Tsong kha pa, *The Great Treatise on the Stages of the Path to Enlightenment*, 3 vols., trans. by Joshua Cutler et al. (Ithaca, NY: Snow Lion Publications, 2000–2004). Tsongkhapa (1357–1419) is, of course, the founder of the Gelug school.

42 Lha mo śramaṇa. This goddess is considered to be an emanation of Tārā. The lineage of dream prognostication based on this deity goes back, in the Gelug school at least, to the time of the First Dalai Lama, Gendün Drub (Dge 'dub grub, 1391–1474).

43 *Shing rta*, fol. 14b.

44 Sgom sde Nam mkha' rgyal mtshan (1532–92) was the eleventh abbot of Sera Jé. The Fifth Dalai Lama states that Khöntön Rinpoché studied under this master in the water-dragon year (1592), i.e., during the last year of Gomdé Rinpoché's life; *Shing rta*, fol. 15a. See also Khöntönpa's remarks on Gomdepa in his *Gzhin rje gshed chos 'byung*, pp. 138–39 and 143–47.

45 Khöntön Rinpoché would in fact write a history of the masters in the Yamāntaka lineage entitled *'Jam dpal gzhin rje gshed skor gyi bla ma brgyud pa'i chos 'byung gdul bya'i re 'dod skong ba yid bzhin nor bu'i phreng ba*, a work that is still extant and that has been recently published by the Library of Tibetan Works and Archives in Dharamsala, mentioned earlier; see also Martin, *Tibetan Histories*, entry 196, p. 99. In his *History* of the lineage, Khöntönpa mentions that he himself received the Yamāntaka teachings from Gomdepa; see the previous note.

46 Chos rje Rin chen bshes gnyen (b. sixteenth century) was a student of Gomdepa (see above), who succeeded his master to the throne of Sera Jé as its twelfth abbot. It may have been due to Gomdepa's passing that Khöntön Rinpoché went to study under Chöje Rinchen Shenyen.

47 Pha bong kha ri khrod. Pabongkha Hermitage is located about two miles west of Sera.

48 Chos rje Dpal 'byor rgya mtsho (d. 1599), the twenty-fifth holder of the Ganden throne, was a teacher of Gomdepa. He became Ganden Tripa (Dga' ldan khri pa) in 1582.

49 Chos rje Dge 'dun rgyal mtshan (1532–1605/7), the twenty-eighth holder of the throne of Ganden Monastery, had ascended to the throne of Tsongkhapa a few years prior to ordaining Khöntön Rinpoché.

50 Dga' ldan rnam par rgyal ba'i gling.

51 Rgyud smad grwa tshang. Khöntönpa himself tells us that he studied at Gyümé for four years beginning in the "sheep year," that is, 1595: *bdag gis lug lo nas lo bzhir chos grwa 'grims; Gzhin rje gshed chos 'byung*, p. 160. He also lists there all of the teachings he received; these are also listed in the Fifth Dalai Lama's *Shing rta*, fols. 16b–17a.

52 Mkhas grub rnam rgyal dpal bzang (1541–1602), also known as Rgyud pa or Rgyud chen Nam mkha' dpal bzang. Khöntön Rinpoché gives a short biography of his master, whom he calls Rdo rje 'chang Rnam rgyal dpal bzang, in *Gzhin rje gzhed chos 'byung*, pp. 157–62.

53 See *Shing rta*, fol. 17b ff., where a variety of masters and teachings are mentioned.

54 'Phyong rgyas. See *Shing rta*, fols. 18b–19a, for an account of Khöntön Rinpoché's reception at Chonggyé.

55 Nyang bran Rin chen tshal pa.

56 These are mentioned in *Shing rta*, fols. 20a–b.

57 *Slob dpon*.

58 Nyi ma thang, a Gelug teaching college of Sangpu (Gsang phu) Monastery founded by Nyalgö Rinchen Samdrub (Gnyal rgod Rin chen bsam grub, fourteenth–fifteenth centuries), a student of Tsongkhapa. Sangpu is located just south of Lhasa. Sde srid, *Baiḍurya Ser po*, p. 148, lists the masters of this college, placing Khöntön Rinpoché between Tsedangwa Ngödrub Gyatso (Rtses dang ba Dgnos grub rgya mtsho) and Gungru Künga Rinchen (Gung ru Kun dga' rin chen). One of Khöntön Rinpoché's own students, Lozang Gyatso (Blo bzang rgya mtsho, b. 1590), also held the seat of Nyima Tang, although much later.

59 Yon tan rgya mtsho (1589–1616).

60 The timing of these appointments is a bit uncertain. *Bla brgyud*, for example, states that he was abbot at Nyima Tang for only a year before becoming abbot of Sera Jé. Dudjom Rinpoché, *The Nyingma School*, vol. 1, p. 678, also mentions that he was a scholar at Tsetang Monastery earlier in his life, though it is unclear when this might have been.

61 *Shing rta*, fol. 21a: *khyad par byes pa'i grub mtha'i dka' gnang[d] thams cad la 'dris par yod pas.*

62 On the fact that early abbots of Sera were usually appointed by their predecessors, see Ary, "Logic, Lives and Lineage," p. 140.

63 *Rdo rje phreng ba*, the explanatory tantra (*bshad rgyud*) of the Guhyasamāja cycle. The date (*lcags phag*) is mentioned by the Fifth Dalai Lama in *Shing rta*, but more importantly, it is mentioned by Khöntönpa himself in *Gzhin rje gshed chos 'byung*, p. 155.

64 Paṇ chen Blo bzang chos kyi rgyal mtshan (1570–1662). Khöntönpa mentions him briefly in his *Gzhin rje gshed chos 'byung*, pp. 148–52.

65 "Lord of Pabongkha" presumably means abbot or head of the hermitage. *Shing rta*, fol. 22a.

66 See *Shing rta*, fols. 24a–b.

67 *Shing rta*, fol. 25a: *thos nor mang yang chog shes ngom pa med.*

68 See *Shing rta*, fol. 25b and also 39a. On a miraculous footprint said to have been left at Ganden by Khöntönpa, see the passage from Tuken's (Thu'u kwan Blo bzang chos kyi nyi ma) biography of Changkya Rinpoché cited by His Holiness the Dalai Lama (October 1977) in "Concerning Dholgyal with reference to the views of past masters and other related matters," http://www.dalailama.com/page.155.htm.

69 See *Shing rta*, fols. 27b–28a, where a certain Rongpa Rabjampa (Rong pa Rab 'byams pa) is specifically mentioned as someone who appears to have found every opportunity to oppose Khöntön Rinpoché. The Fifth Dalai Lama compares this to the opposition that the translator Kawa Peltseg (Ska ba dpal rtsegs, ninth century) faced at the hands of jealous ministers at the time that he invited the Indian master Vimalamitra to Tibet. The comparison must have seemed especially appropriate to the Great Fifth because he considered Khöntön Rinpoché a reincarnation of that translator.

70 Rin spungs pa.

71 The initial shift of power from the Rinpung to the Tsang kings took place in 1565, when Karma Tseten Dorjé (Karma Tshe brtan rdo rje) seized Shigatsé from the Rinpungpa and took control of Tsang. See Ahmad, *Sino-Tibetan Relations*, p. 94; and Sørenson and Hazod, *Rulers of the Celestial Plain*, p. 55. But the final turning point in this political transition probably did not take place until 1612, at which point the armies of Tsang had conquered all of northern and western Tibet as well as Gyantsé (Rgyal rtse) and Neudong (Sne'u gdong); see Ahmad, *Sino-Tibetan Relations*, p. 101.

72 Gtsang pa sde srid.

73 For example, in 1605, the very year that Khöntön Rinpoché became master of the Jé College, or perhaps in 1607, Tsangpa troops put down a revolt by the Pagmodrupas in Kyishö. Despite being nominally in control of central Tibet, the Tsang kings were also aware of the threat posed by the presence

of Mongolian troops in the capital and had to turn their armies back at least once (in 1610) in their invasions of central Tibet; Ahmad, *Sino-Tibetan Relations*, p. 101.

74 See Sde srid, *Baiḍurya ser po*, p. 132. See also *Tibetan Chronological Tables*, p. 220.

75 Karma Bstan skyong dbang po (d. 1642), the son of Karma Püntsog Wangyel.

76 Stag lung tshe. See Ahmad, *Sino-Tibetan Relations*, pp. 103–4.

77 Mnga' ri. See *Tibetan Chronological Tables*, p. 221.

78 Yer pa.

79 See *Shing rta*, fols. 29b–30a. Khöntönpa mentions in passing in his *Gzhin rje gshed chos 'byung*, p. 36, that he is unable to write a portion of his history because the required text "was destroyed in the war": *dpe cha dmag gi dus thor bas 'bri ma nus.*

80 *Shing rta*, fol. 28a, states that outwardly Khöntön Rinpoché appeared to come to this decision after doing some divinations but that in fact the master simply knew that the time to step down had arrived.

81 It was as a result of his long stay at Pabongkha that Khöntön Rinpoché is also known under the title Pabongkhapa (Pha bong kha pa). Although some contemporary scholars have claimed that the controversial Pabongkhapa Dechen Nyingpo (Pha bong kha pa Bde chen snying po, 1878–1941) was Khöntönpa's reincarnation, this is a misunderstanding. Dechen Nyingpo was identified in his lifetime as the reincarnation of a minor abbot (*mkhan sprul*). He in fact never lived at Pabongkha but rather meditated for a period of time at the nearby hermitage of Rtags brtan sgrub phug. It was the Changkya lamas (see appendix 2) who were considered the reincarnations of Khöntönpa.

On a prophecy found in the *Rgyal po bka' thang* mentioning a certain Pha bong kha pa, which the Fifth Dalai Lama sees as referring to Khöntön Rinpoché, see *Shing rta*, fol. 4b. Khöntön Rinpoché penned a small history or "inventory" of the Pabongkha Hermitage, the *Chos kyi rgyal po srong btsan sgam po'i sgrub gnas pha bong kha byang chub shing gi nags khrod kyi dkar chag*, which seems to have been available to the author of (and incorporated into) a modern-day inventory of the monastery; see José Ignacio Cabezón, *The Hermitages of Sera* (Charlottesville: Tibetan and Himalayan Digital Library, 2006), http://www.thdl.org/collections/cultgeo/mons/sera/hermitages/pdfs/sera_herm_pabongkha.pdf. See also the Fifth Dalai Lama's remarks about the hermitage in *Shing rta*, fols. 30a ff. Khöntönpa's *Gzhin rje gshed chos 'byung* (pp. 141, 147) makes it clear that at least two other individuals—Deleg Nyima and Gomdé Namkha Gyeltsen—retired to Pabongkha after their terms as abbot of the Jé College. By the time of Khöntönpa, therefore, this might already have been something of an established tradition.

82   *Shing rta*, fol. 30a: *de nas sgrub pa 'ba' zhig la thugs gzhol.*

83   For a list of some of his main practices during this period, see *Shing rta*, fol. 31a.

84   For instance, Mongolian and Tsangpa troops fought at Kyang Tang Gang (Skyang thang sgang), just southeast of Drepung, in 1620 or 1621. The war spread to Lhasa. The Mongol supporters of the Gelugpas seized the city and drove out the forces of Tsang. Under a truce negotiated by the Penchen Rinpoché, a truce that saved many Tsangpa troops from slaughter at the hands of the Mongols, the Gelug institutions in central Tibet regained much of their previous power and property. But the political tension between Tsang and central Tibet would continue for another two decades. See *Tibetan Chronological Tables*, p. 223. As Sørenson and Hazod, *Rulers of the Celestial Plain*, p. 55, make clear, the Mongolian troops were supported by Kyishöpa (Skyid shod pa) and other pro-Gelug Tibetan forces.

85   Zur chen Chos dbyings rang grol, or Zur Dpal 'byor phrin las rab rgyas (1604–69), was an important holder of many Nyingma lineages who was himself one of the teachers of the Fifth Dalai Lama. Zurchen studied under Khöntön Rinpoché from 1621 to 1637, often receiving two daily teaching sessions from his master. *Gu bkra*, p. 300, and *Bdud 'joms*, p. 338 (Dudjom Rinpoché, *The Nyingma School*, p. 678), both state that Khöntön Rinpoché taught Yungtönpa's (G.yung ston Rdo rje dpal ba, 1284–1365) commentary on the *Guhyagarbha* as well as the *seminal essence* instructions to Zurchen. It was due to his training under Khöntön Rinpoché, our sources tell us, that Zurchen was able to defend Nyingma tantric exegesis at Tsetang Monastery during lectures he gave there in 1624. Interestingly, Zurchen is also considered the next lineage lama following Khöntön Rinpoché in the Gelug lineage of masters of the *lamrim* tradition. On the teachings Khöntön Rinpoché gave to Zurchen, see *Shing rta*, fol. 33a. See also *Bla brgyud*, pp. 796ff.; as well as Sørensen and Hazod, *Rulers of the Celestial Plain*, p. 44 et passim.

86   See Sde srid, *Baiḍurya ser po*, p. 382.

87   With the enthronement of the Great Fifth at Drepung, many Mongolian pilgrims began to arrive in Lhasa. The large numbers of Mongolians in Lhasa worried the king of Tsang, who, given the events of the previous year, saw

these foreigners as a threat. See Ahmad, *Sino-Tibetan Relations*, p. 109.

88 These are listed in *Shing rta*, fol. 35b. They include practices of both the Nyingma and the New schools.

89 Sde srid Sangs rgyas rgya mtsho (1635–1705).

90 Sde srid, *Baiḍurya ser po*, p. 384: *sku tshe'i stod kyi yongs 'dzin gyi gtso bo yin zhes yang yang gsung.*

91 *Shing rta*, fol. 38a.

92 *Shing rta*, fol. 38b: *rje 'di zhal bzhugs skabs/ ris med chos la mkhyen pa che bas grub mtha' mi gtsang bar gleng mkhan mang po yod de/ grub mtha' gtsang mo tshos [tshod] kyang/ rgyal ba tsong kha pa'i bstan pa la thugs zhen bcos min rje 'di pa tsam dga' bar mchis/.*

93 *Gzhin rje gshed chos 'byung*, p. 195.

94 *Shing rta*, fol. 39a: *bka' chos kyi 'tshams la gsung 'phros kyi rigs sngon 'byon gyi lo rgyus/ rgan rabs kyi ngag sgros kyis mtha' brten pa ma gtogs rgyu mtshan dang mi 'brel ba'i dug gsum gyis kun nas bslang pa'i long gtam gsung ba ni ma thos/.*

95 *Shing rta*, fol. 39a.

96 'Phan yul rgyal lha khang. See Ahmad, *Sino-Tibetan Relations*, pp. 114–15.

97 *Shing rta*, fol. 40a.

98 *Shing rta*, fol. 40a: *rang dbang 'dus pa zhig dka' bar 'dug kyang/ rgya hor dbus gtsang sogs su skye ba len 'dod ni med ces bka' phebs/ de yang thugs dbang mi 'dus pa sogs ni dgongs pa can du nges shing/.*

99 These events are recounted in *Shing rta*, fols. 40b–41a.

100 *Shing rta*, fol. 41b: *de la dgongs gzhi che ba yod tshod du 'dug kyang 'di zhes brjod pa'i yul las 'das.*

101 *Shing rta*, fol. 42a: *'chi ba 'od gsal chos kyi sku las bar do longs spyod rdzogs skur bzhengs pa'i rtags su thugs dam grol.*

102 For a precise description of these services, see *Shing rta*, fol. 42b.

103 Dudjom Rinpoché, *The Nyingma School*, vol. 1, p. 679, gives the exact date of his death as August 30, 1637. Sde srid's *Baiḍurya ser po*, p. 144, lists four abbots of Pabongkha after Khöntön Rinpoché: Zhal snga nas Dpal 'byor rab rgyas, Se ra pa 'Jam dbyangs grags pa, Mkhan Ngag dbang bstan 'dzin, and Smad bla zur Blo bzang don grub.

104 Gushri Khan, the leader of the Koshot Mongols who was responsible for the final triumph of the Gelugpas over their Tsangpa/Kagyü rivals a few years later, was secretly visiting Lhasa at the time. The Fifth Dalai Lama tells us that the Koshot ruler witnessed Khöntön Rinpoché's body in equipoise after he stopped breathing.

105 The Dalai Lama himself speaks of commissioning the stūpa. But the statue

(*sman sku*) of Khöntön Rinpoché is only mentioned by Sde srid, *Baiḍurya ser po*, p. 417.

106 *Pha bong kha'i dkar chag* (hand-copy of an "inventory" of the hermitage made available to me in Lhasa, 2004), fol. 44b. This work, as mentioned above, seems to incorporate into its early sections portions of Khöntön Rinpoché's own inventory of the hermitage. Sde srid, *Baiḍurya ser po*, p. 417, lists the various ways in which the Fifth Dalai Lama endowed Pabongkha after his teacher's death.

107 Among Khöntön Rinpoché's other Gelug students was Drungpa Tsöndrü Gyeltsen (Drung pa Brtson 'grus rgyal mtshan, seventeenth century), a pivotal figure in the Sera hermitage tradition, as I have argued in my *Hermitages of Sera*, p. 16.

108 *Lta ba.*

109 *Sgom.*

110 Zhabs drung Mi 'gyur rdo rje, *Phyag rgya chen po las 'phros pa'i rang lan rtsod pa'i mun sel*, in Gsung 'bum (New Delhi: Ngawang Toppgay, 1981), pp. 534–35.

111 *Grub mtha'*; Sanskrit, *siddhānta.*

112 *Shan 'byed pa.*

113 *Dgag len*; see my introduction to José Ignacio Cabezón and Geshe Lobsang Dargyay, *Freedom from Extremes: Gorampa's "Distinguishing the Views" and the Polemics of Emptiness* (Boston: Wisdom Publications, 2006).

114 *Dbu ma chen po.*

115 Khöntön Rinpoché mentions some of these other systems in the colophon to his text: the Pacifier (Zhiché), the Practice of Severance (Chöyul), the Six-limbed Yoga of the Kālacakra Tantra (Jordrug), and the Six Dharmas of Nāropa (Chödrug).

116 Mi la ras pa, *Mi la'i mgur 'bum* (Gangtok: Sherab Gyaltsen, 1983), p. 728.

117 *Gcod.*

118 See Sarah Harding, *Machik's Complete Enlightenment* (Ithaca, NY: Snow Lion Publications, 2003), pp. 114–15.

119 The lines are found in the Third Karmapa's famous *Mahāmudrā Prayer* (*Nges don phyag rgya chen po'i smon lam*); cited in Mdo sngags chos kyi rgya mtsho, *Phyag rdzogs dbu gsum gyi lta ba'i dris lan mkhas pa'i zhal lung*, in *Gsang sngags gsar rnying gi lta ba'i rnam bzhag legs bshad gces btus* (Dharamsala: Rnam rgyal grwa tshang shes yon lhan tshogs, 2009), pp. 137–38. I would like to thank His Holiness the Dalai Lama for making this publication available to me.

120 Klong chen pa, *Rdzogs pa chen po bsam gtan ngal gso* (Reprint of the A 'dzom 'brug pa chos sgar xylographs, 1999), TBRC W23760, vol. 3, fols. 12a–b.

121 Indeed, Khöntönpa does not claim originality, clearly stating that this synthetic and ecumenical approach is part of a lineage of preliminary practices of the *seminal essence (nying thig)* tradition, a lineage that he states comes down to him from Sanggyé Tsöndrü. (See the colophon to the text.)

122 *Dge ldan bka' brgyud rin po che'i bka' srol kyi phyag chen rtsa ba,* together with a commentary (*rgyas bshad*). The root text has been translated by Alexander Berzin and commented upon by His Holiness the Dalai Lama in His Holiness the Dalai Lama and Alexander Berzin, *The Gelug/Kagyü Tradition of Mahamudra* (Ithaca, NY: Snow Lion Publications, 1997). Since the colophon of Penchen Rinpoché's text does not tell us when it was composed, we do not know whether it was written before or after the work of Khöntön Rinpoché.

123 Paṇ chen Blo bzang chos kyi rgyal mtshan, *Dge ldan bka' brgyud rin po che'i bka' srol kyi phyag chen rtsa ba,* Gsung 'bum (Collected Works), vol. 4 (*nga*), pp. 82–83. The Penchen Lama's words in this passage should not be taken to mean that he was unaware of differences that existed between the views of his own and other schools, or that he never critiqued the views of other scholars. For example, we know that he wrote at least one important polemical work directed at Tagtsang Lotsawa (Stag tshang lo tsā ba Shes rab rin chen, b. 1405), one of the earliest critics of Tsongkhapa. See José I. Cabezón, "On the *Grwa pa rin chen pa'i rtsod len* of Paṇ chen bLo bzang chos rgyan," *Asiatische Studien/Études Asiatiques* 49.4 (1995): 643–69.

124 Lama Zhang (Bla ma zhang, 1123–93), whom Khöntön Rinpoché quotes extensively in his work, states in his *Phyag rgya chen po lam khyer* (*Making Mahāmudrā into the Path*), Gsung 'bum, vol. 3 (*ga*), p. 516:

> There are various names for
> the many forms of meditation [on reality],
> like *meditating without examples (dpe med pa yi sgom pa)*
> and *meditating on the great reality in intervals (res 'ga' chos nyid chen po bsgom).*
> But although labeled differently,
> I understand that they are not different in their meaning.
> Why get worked up over mere names?
> It is not right to have doubts
> about those who meditate in these different ways.

Shortly after Khöntön Rinpoché, Tselé Natsog Rangdröl (Rtse le Sna tshogs rang grol, b. 1608) attempted a reconciliation of Mahāmudrā, Dzogchen, and Madhyamaka. Urgyen Tulku et al., *Quintessential Dzogchen*, 206–7, translate a section from the work of Tselé Natsog Rangdröl, where he states, "In the ultimate sense there is no difference between Mahamudra and Dzogchen.... The authentic great Kagyü masters took self-cognizant mindfulness as their practice, which is identical to the primordially pure self-awareness of the Dzogchen system. Thus, despite differences in terminology, there is no difference in their meaning." Tselepa also has a small text entitled *The Practice of the View and Meditation in Mahāmudrā, Dzogchen, and Madhyamaka* (*Phyag rdzogs dbu gsum gyi lta sgom nyams len*) in his Gsung 'bum (New Delhi: Sanji Dorje, 1974), vol. 2, pp. 89–137, but I have yet to examine this work.

Shortly after Tselé Natsog Rangdröl, the aforementioned Nyingma scholar Zhabdrung Mingyur Dorjé, in a work called *Dispelling the Darkness of Disputations: My Own Response [to Questions] Related to Mahāmudrā* (*Phyag rgya chen po las 'phros pa'i rang lan rtsod pa'i mun sel*), attempted to show that the view found in the writing of the great Kagyü masters was not inconsistent with Dzogchen. Even in the twentieth century we find scholars writing in this vein—scholars like Do Ngag Chökyi Gyatso (Mdo sngags chos kyi rgya mtsho, 1903–57), who penned several works very similar to the work of Khöntönpa translated here; see the first several titles in his *Snyan dgon sprul sku gsung rab pa'i gsung rtsom bces bsgrigs* (Zi ling: Mtsho sngon mi rigs dpe skrun khang, 1996).

125   Mdo sngags chos kyi rgya mtso, *Phyag rdzogs dbu gsum gyi lta ba'i dris lan mkhas pa'i zhal lung*, pp. 127–28. This great scholar is not unaware of the fact that there are passages in the writings of Rongzom Chöjé (Rong zom chos rje, b. eleventh century) that suggest that the view of the inner tantras is superior to (and therefore different from) the Madhyamaka (see pp. 128–30 of Do Ngag Chökyi Gyatso's text), but he attributes this to the fact that at the time of Rongzompa, a clear distinction had yet to be made between Svātantrika and Prāsaṅgika Madhyamaka. On the question of Rongzom's position vis-à-vis the Madhyamaka, see also Heidi I. Køppl, *Establishing Appearances as Divine: Rongzom Chokyi Zangpo on Reasoning, Madhyamaka, and Purity* (Ithaca, NY: Snow Lion Publications, 2008).

126   Rgyal tshab Dar ma rin chen (1364–1432), Tsongkhapa's eldest student and his successor on the throne of Ganden Monastery.

127   *Bstan bcos mngon par rtogs pa'i rgyan gyi 'grel ṭik rnam bshad snying po'i rgyan gyi tshig don rab gsal*, mentioned at http://www.chibs.edu.tw/publication/

chbj/02/chbj0205.htm, and at http://www.aciprelease.org/r6web/flat/
R0008F_E.TXT, where his name is incorrectly spelled Mkhon ston. The
work has apparently been published in India.

128 *Bde smon rnam bshad*. In the collection of the Tibetan Buddhist Resource
Center, TBRC W1CZ1111; the text was scanned from a microfilm copy of
a blockprint of unknown origin.

129 *'Jam dpal gshin rje gshed skor gyi bla ma brgyud pa'i chos 'byung gdul bya'i re 'dod
skong ba yid bzhin nor bu'i 'phreng ba* (Dharamsala: Library of Tibetan Works
and Archives, 2005).

130 'Khon btsun (sic) dpal 'byor lhun grub, *Dkon mchog gsum la skyabs su 'gro
tshul gyi gdams pa zab mo snyan bgryud khyad par gsum ldan* (Beijing, 19??).
The work is listed as the sixteenth title in twenty-two folios in a collection of
miscellaneous texts in the East Asia Library at the University of California,
Berkeley, EAL.Tib.169.

131 We know that Khöntön Rinpoché became abbot of the Jé College of Sera
in 1605 at the age of forty-four and that he left for Pabongkha in 1619. He
mentions writing the work in question in "the abbatial household of the Jé
College (Byes bla brang) in a 'bird' year." Only one bird year falls between
1605 and 1619, and that is the year 1609. Khöntön Rinpoché was forty-eight
years old at this point. *Shing rta*, fol. 31b, mentions that Khöntön Rinpoché
gave teachings on this work at Ganden around the year 1622, when he was
sixty-one.

132 'Bri gung skyabs mgon, *Bka' brgyud mgur mtsho*, p. 208.

133 This translation is based on an edition of the Tibetan text, *Snyan brgyud yid
bzhin nor bu lta ba spyi khyab tu ngo sprod pa'i khrid yig*, found in *Sngags rdzogs
dbu ma'i skor gyi dpe dkon thor bu'i rigs phyogs bsgrigs* (Bla rung sgar: Gser
ljongs bla ma rung lnga rig nang bstan slob grwa chen mo, 2005). The page
numbers of this edition have been interpolated within the translation for easy
reference. The title of the text in the modern edition is slightly different from
that found in the catalog of Khöntön Peljor Lhündrub's collected works mentioned in the list of *Teachings Received* (*Thob yig*), a work found in the Collected Works of the Fifth Dalai Lama, where the title of the text is *Lta ba spyi
khyab tu ngo sprod pa'i tshul gsal bar byed pa snyan brgyud yid bzhin nor bu*.

134 Rdo rje chos, a peaceful form of Vajrapāṇi.

135 The editor of the modern edition corrects the text's "Rtsam por" to "Sgam
por." Even if this were an accurate emendation, however, it is uncertain which
of the many figures known under the name "Sgam po" the editor has in mind,
though one might suspect that it is Gampopa, Milarepa's disciple.

136 *Nying thig* is a tradition of Dzogchen teachings of the Nyingma school. The form most commonly practiced today, the Seminal Essence of the Great Expanse (*Klong chen snying thig*), was systematized by Jigmé Lingpa ('Jigs med gling pa, 1729–98). Given that the latter flourished long after our author, however, what Khöntön Rinpoché has in mind here is an earlier *nyingtig*, perhaps the Fourfold Seminal Essence (*Snying thig ya bzhi*) compiled by Longchenpa (Klong chen pa, 1308–64), a figure whom Khöntönpa quotes several times in this text; or perhaps he means the Seminal Essence of the Ḍākinīs (*Mkha' 'gro snying thig*), revealed by Pema Ledrel Tsel (Padma las 'brel rtsal, b. 1248); or the Seminal Essence of the Clear Expanse (*Klong gsal snying thig*), revealed by Ratna Lingpa (Ratna gling pa, 1403–79), a cycle of revealed treasure teachings that Khöntönpa's biographers specifically mention among the teachings he received (see note 7).

137 Such histories of the lineage are, of course, found in a variety of sources. A very brief one, specific to the *nyingtig* tradition, can be found in a work of the Third Dzogchen Rinpoché, Ngedön Tendzin Zangpo (Nges don Bstan 'dzin bzang po, 1759–92), *Rdzogs pa chen po mkha' 'gro snying thig gi khrid yig thar lam bgrod byed shing rta bzang po* (Chengdu: Mi rigs dpe skrun khang, 1997), pp. 194–96, 248–54, 258–68. A history of the lineage of Ratna Lingpa's Clear Expanse revelations is found in his *Klong gsal snying thig gi brgyud pa'i lo rgyus*, Gsung 'bum (Darjeeling: Taklung Tsetrul Pema Wangyal, 1977–79), vol. *da*, pp. 23–26. See also Dudjom Rinpoche, *The Nyingma School of Tibetan Buddhism*. There are, of course, similar lineage histories of the Mahāmudrā and Madhyamaka traditions.

138 See, for example, Gampopa, *The Jewel Ornament of Liberation*, trans. by Khenpo Konchog Gyaltsen and Ani K. Trinlay Chödron (Ithaca, NY: Snow Lion Publications, 1998); Tsong kha pa, *Great Treatise*; and Patrul Rinpoche, *The Words of My Perfect Teacher*, trans. by Padmakara Translation Group (San Francisco: HarperCollins, 1998).

139 Empowerment (Skt. *abhiṣeka*, Tib. *dbang*), a ritual procedure where the master introduces the disciple to the palace or *maṇḍala* of the deity, or in some instances introduces the disciple to the nature of his or her own mind. Empowerment is the entryway into tantric practice. See H. H. the Dalai Lama, Tsong-kha-pa, and Jeffrey Hopkins, *Tantra in Tibet* (Ithaca, NY: Snow Lion Publications, 1987).

140 Vows are of three types: the vows of individual liberation (*pratimokṣa*), the bodhisattva vows, and the tantric vows. See Sakya Pandita Kunga Gyaltshen, *A Clear Differentiation of the Three Codes*, trans. by Jared Rhoton and Victoria

M. Scott (Albany: State University of New York Press, 2002). In addition, many of the traditions described in this work have their own sets of commitments. For example, Bla ma zhang, *Tai lo chos drug* (*The Six Dharmas of Tilopa*), in the "Nyams len sgom khrid" section of his Gsung 'bum (Kathmandu: Gam-po-pa Library, 2004), vol. 3 (*ga*), fol. 6a, describes the four special commitments associated with the practice of Mahāmudrā: "Not trying to abandon afflictions, since they are your own mind. Not relying on antidotes within the continuum of gnosis, since they [gnosis and the antidotes] are not two. Not meditating on reality, since it is not an object. Cherishing no hope of a result, since it is the realization of the nature of mind."

141 Vajrasattva practice (which includes the recitation of the hundred-syllable mantra) is a form of purification meditation. See Lama Thubten Yeshe, *Becoming Vajrasattva: The Tantric Path of Purification*, ed. Nicholas Ribush, 2nd ed. (Boston: Wisdom Publications, 2004).

142 Normally written *kusali*, this is a visualization/ritual practice in which the adept offers his or her own body to buddhas or deities. The practice is related to the famous Tibetan tradition known as Severance mentioned earlier. See Patrul Rinpoche, *The Words of My Perfect Teacher*, pp. 297ff.

143 The yoga of the spiritual master is the ritual/meditative practice where one comes to regard the spiritual master as an enlightened being and unites the master's mind with his or her own.

144 The text's *tshang btsal ba* has been emended to read *mtshang btsal ba*.

145 The text's *nges pa byang ba* has been emended to read *nges pa byung ba*.

146 Buddhas are free from the fault, or extreme, of existence because they are no longer subject to involuntary rebirth. They are free from the fault of "peace" because they do not enter the personal peace of arhatship, but rather work for the sake of all sentient beings until samsara has been emptied.

147 Saraha, *Dohakośamahāmudropadeśa, Do ha mdzod ces bya ba phyag rgya chen po'i man ngag*, Sde dge Bstan 'gyur, Toh. no. 2273, Rgyud *shi*, fol. 122a. Saraha continues:

> Everything that appears to us as an instance of mind or phenomena
> cannot be found when searched for, nor does the searcher exist.
> Since what is nonexistent does not arise or cease in the three times,
> it does not change into anything else.
> That is the reality of essential great bliss.
> Hence, all appearances are the dharma body;
> all sentient beings are buddhas;

all composite actions are, from the beginning, the sphere of reality
(*dharmadhātu*);
and all imagined phenomena (*btags pa'i chos*) are like the horns of a
rabbit. (fol. 122b)

Similar verses are found in, e.g., Niguma's *Great Seal of Self-Liberation* (*Rang
grol phyag rgya chen po*): *snang grag chos rnams rang gi sems/ sems las ma gtogs
chos gzhan med/*; see Miranda Shaw, *Passionate Enlightenment* (Princeton:
Princeton University Press, 1994), pp. 88 and 224. In the classical Tibetan
sources, Saraha is considered the teacher of Nāgārjuna. For a study of this
important figure, see Kurtis Schaeffer, *Dreaming the Great Brahmin: Tibetan
Traditions of the Buddhist Poet-Saint Saraha* (Oxford: Oxford University
Press, 2005).

148 The lines are found in Saraha, *Dohakośa*; see Schaeffer, *Dreaming the Great
Brahmin*, p. 147; and Roger R. Jackson, *Tantric Treasures: Three Collections of
Mystical Verse from Buddhist India* (Oxford: Oxford University Press, 2004),
p. 73.

149 The "three worlds" are the three realms of Buddhist cosmology: the desire,
form, and formless realms.

150 *Daśabhūmikasūtra, Sa bcu pa'i mdo*; Sde dge Bka' 'gyur, Toh. no. 44, Phal
chen *kha*, fol. 220b. The passage is also found in the *Pratyutpannabuddha-
saṃmukkhāvasthitasamādhisūtra*; see Paul Harrison, *The Tibetan Text of the
Prtayutapanna-Buddha-Saṃmukhāvasthita-Samādhi Sūtra*, Studia Philologica
Buddhica Monograph Series, no. 1 (Tokyo: The Reiyukai Library, 1978),
p. 36: *khams gsum pa 'di dag ni sems tsam mo*. See also Paul Williams, *Critical Concepts in Religious Studies* (London: Routledge, 2006), pp. 249–50 and
254n47.

151 Khöntön Rinpoché states that this is a teaching of the Lord (Jo bo rje), a
title usually understood to refer to Atiśa, but the technique (and the verse)
appears to have its origin in a text usually attributed to Atiśa's teacher,
Serlingpa (Gser gling pa, fl. tenth century). Gser gling pa, *Sems dpa'i rim
pa* (*The Stages of the Heroic Mind*), preserved in a collection of mind-
training texts by Dkon mchog rgyal mtshan, the *Blo sbyong brgya rtsa*; *Blo
sbyong brgya rtsa dang dkar chag gdungs sel zla ba* (Dharamsala: Shes rig par
khang, 1973), pp. 128–29. The authorship of this text, however, has been
questioned; see Thupten Jinpa, *Mind Training*, p. 181, verse 24, and pp.
599–600n303.

152 The "object of negation" is the object of innate ignorance, the thing that must

be negated through analysis in order to come to an understanding of the ultimate truth.

153 "Concordant and discordant conditions" may refer to the conditions that contribute to or impede the enemy's flourishing as a human being, or more specifically that contribute to or detract from his or her status as an enemy.

154 *Śrāvakas*, "disciples," or literally "hearers," are followers of the Lesser Vehicle (Hīnayāna), who at the beginning of their spiritual journey focus on the observance of the vows of the monastic discipline.

155 In the *generation* or *creation stage* (*bskyed rim*), adepts learn to perfect the visualization in which they are first transformed into emptiness and then emerge from that emptiness in the form of the deity, a practice known as *deity yoga* (*lha'i rnal 'byor*); see H. H. The Dalai Lama et al., *Tantra in Tibet*; Jigme Lingpa, Patrul Rinpoche, and Getse Mahapandita, *Deity, Mantra, and Wisdom: The Development Stage in Tibetan Buddhist Tantra*, trans. by Dharmacakra Translation Committee (Ithaca, NY: Snow Lion Publications, 2006); Gyatrul Rinpoche, *The Generation Stage in Buddhist Tantra* (Ithaca, NY: Snow Lion Publications, 1996); and Jamgön Kongtrül, *Creation and Completion: Essential Points of Tantric Meditation*, trans. by Sarah Harding with a commentary by Khenchen Thrangu Rinpoche (Boston: Wisdom Publications, 1996).

156 Once the practice of the generation stage has been perfected, adepts move to the *completion* or *perfection stage* (*rdzogs rim*), practices involving the subtle physiology of the human body, which consists of channels, wind energies, and drops. See Daniel Cozort, *Highest Yoga Tantra* (Ithaca, NY: Snow Lion Publications, 2005), part III.

157 Padmasambhava, *Padma bka' thang* (Chengdu: Mi rigs dpe skrung khang, 1996), p. 644; see also Gustave-Charles Toussaint, *Le Dict de Padma: Padma Thang Yig, Ms. de Litang* (Paris: Librairie Ernst Leroux, 1933), p. 435.

158 Padampa Sanggyé (Pha Dam pa sangs rgyas, b. eleventh century), the founder of the Zhi byed, "Pacifier," meditative system.

159 Our text's *thog rdugs* has been emended to read *thog brdugs*, but see the following note.

160 These two lines are from Padampa Sanggyé's famous "One Hundred Verses of Advice to the People of Dingri" (*Zhal gdams ding ri brgya rtsa ma*): *stong pa'i ngang du rig pa'i mdung bskor gyis/ lta bar thogs thug med do ding ri ba*, which varies slightly from the citation in our text.

161 Śāntideva (fl. eighth century), the great Indian saint who authored *Entering the Bodhisattva Practice* (*Bodhicaryāvatāra*).

162 Śāntideva, *Bodhicaryāvatāra*, 9:140, *Byang chub sems dpa' spyod pa la 'jug pa*, Sde dge Bstan 'gyur, Toh. no. 3871, Dbu ma *la*, fol. 36a. On these lines, see Paul Williams, *Altruism and Reality: Studies in the Philosophy of the Bodhicaryāvatāra* (London: RoutledgeCurzon, 1997), pp. 65ff.

163 The aggregates are the physical and mental constituents of the person—the body and the various aspects of the mind.

164 Candrakīrti (seventh century), *Madhyamakāvatāra*, 6:120; Louis de la Vallée Poussin, ed., *Madhyamakāvatāra par Candrakīrti* (St. Petersbourg: Imprimerie de l'Académie Impériale des Sciences, 1912), p. 233; *Dbu ma la 'jug pa*, Sde dge Bstan 'gyur, Toh. no. 3861, Dbu ma *'a*, fol. 210a. See also C. W. Huntington, trans., *The Emptiness of Emptiness* (Honolulu: University of Hawaii Press, 1989), p. 171.

165 Candrakīrti, *Madhyamakāvatāra*, 6:117c; Sde dge, fol. 210a; La Vallée Poussin, *Madhyamakāvatāra*, p. 230; Huntington, *Emptiness of Emtiness*, p. 171.

166 Perhaps a reference to the melding of the mother and son clear lights (*ma dang bu'i 'od gsal*). But see also Padmasambhava, *Padma bka' thang*, p. 645, where it speaks of the nonduality of mother and son and the merging of appearances and emptiness (*ma bu gnyis med…snang stong gnyis med bsres*).

167 *Clear Expanse* (*Klong gsal*) is the name of one of the seventeen tantras of the Dzogchen tradition. The lines that follow, however, are not found in the tantra by this name in the Collected Tantras of the Nyingma (Rnying ma rgyud 'bum, Mtshams brag no. Tb. 270). It is not clear, therefore, which text is being cited here.

168 *Dkon brtsegs* = *Ratnakūṭa[sūtra]*, an important early Mahāyāna collection. However, the lines actually appear to be from the *Mdo dgongs 'dus*, the chief scripture of the Anuyoga section of the nine vehicles, Sde dge bka' 'gyur, Toh. no. 829, Rnying rgyud *ka*, fol. 104a.

169 I have yet to locate these exact lines. But similar passages from the same sūtra collection are cited in Dagpo Trashi Namgyel (Dwags po Bkra shis rnam rgyal, 1512–87), *Phyag chen sgom rim zla ba'i 'od zer* (Mtsho sngon: Mi rigs dpe skrung khang, 2001); translated in Takpo Tashi Namgyal, *Mahāmudrā: The Quintessence of Mind and Meditation* (Delhi: Motilal, 2001), pp. 187–88. A similar passage is also quoted in Kamalaśīla's *Bodhicittabhāvana*, Sde dge Bstan 'gyur, Toh. no. 3913, Dbu ma *ki*, fol. 18a [full text = fols. 16b–19a]: *gsang ba pa'i bdag po sems ni de bzhin gshegs pa dgra bcom pa yang dag par rdzogs pa'i sangs rgyas rnams kyis ma gzigs mi gzigs gzigs par mi 'gyur ro/… gsang ba pa'i bdag po sems ni nang na ma yin phyi rol na ma yin gnyis ka'i bar na yang mi dmigs na/ de ci ltar 'dzin par 'gyur/ de ltar na gzung ba dang 'dzin*

pa dang bral ba'o/. Finally, similar lines (in verse) are found in Nāgārjuna's *Bodhicittavivaraṇa,* verse 43; Christian Lindtner, *Nagarjuniana* (Copenhagen: Akademisk Forlag, 1982), p. 198.

170 These lines are not found in either of Śāntideva's two major works—the *Bodhicaryāvatāra* and the *Śikṣāsamuccaya*—nor are they found in the various minor works attributed to him in the Tengyur.

171 Khöntön Rinpoché uses one set of metaphors for the different degrees of concentration he is about to explain. Another, similar set is found in Tilopa's *Mahāmudropadeśa, Phyag rgya chen po man ngag (Instructions on the Great Seal),* Sde dge Bstan 'gyur, Toh. no. 2303, Rgyud *zhi,* fol. 243b: "For the beginner it is like rapids. For the intermediate [adept it is like] the gently flowing Ganges. And for the advanced one, it is like the contact of the mother and son streams."

172 The lines are found in Milarepa's *Collected Songs;* Mi la ras pa, *Mi la'i mgur 'bum* (Gangtok: Sherab Gyaltsen, 1983), p. 387. The version found in Khöntön Rinpoché's text varies slightly from that found in the *Mgur 'bum.* Rechungpa (Ras chung Rdo rje grags pa, 1085–1161) was one of Milarepa's chief disciples.

173 Zhang g.yu grags pa Brtson 'grus grags pa (1123–93), a student of Gampopa and the founder of the Tselpa (Tshal pa) branch of the Kagyü school. He established the famous monastery of Tsel Gungtang (Tshal gung thang) near Lhasa.

174 When, as in this case, I have been unable to find the source of a citation, the quote is left unannotated.

175 Maitripa or Advayavajra, one of the eighty-four great adepts (*mahāsiddha*) of India, was born at the end of the tenth century. He was a student of Nāropa and a teacher of the Tibetan translator Marpa. See Mark Tatz, "The Life of the Siddha Philosopher Maitri Gupta," *Journal of American Oriental Society* 107.4 (1987): 695–711; and H. Hadano, "A Historical Study in the Problems Concerning the Diffusion of Tantric Buddhism in India: Advayavajra, alias Mnaḥ-bdag-Maitripā," in *Religious Studies in Japan,* T. Ishizu et al., eds., pp. 287–99 (Tokyo: Maruzen Co., 1959). Tibetan accounts of his life are found in a variety of sources, including the writings of Padma dkar po, Dpa' bo tsug lag phreng ba, and Tāranātha. See *Tāranātha's Bka'.babs.bdun.ldan: The Seven Instruction Lineages by Jo.nang. Tāranātha,* trans. and ed. by David Templeman (Dharamsala: Library of Tibetan Works and Archives, 1983), pp. 11–14; and Karl Brunnhölz, *Straight from the Heart: Buddhist Pith Instructions* (Ithaca, NY: Snow Lion Publications, 2007), pp. 125ff.

176 See Nālandā Translation Committee, *The Life of Marpa the Translator* (Boston: Shambhala, 1982), p. 30, where this verse is found.

177 *Mi la'i mgur 'bum*, p. 726; Garma C. C. Chang, trans., *The Hundred Thousand Songs of Milarepa* (Boston: Shambhala, 1999), p. 578.

178 Yang dgon pa Rgyal mtshan dpal (1213–58), a famous master of the Drugpa Kagyü tradition, was a student of Götsangpa (Rgod tshangs pa, 1189–1258).

179 *Mi la'i mgur 'bum*, p. 671.

180 Ibid.

181 Bla ma zhang, *Tai lo pa'i chos drug*, fol. 3a, states: "'Destruction of conceptualization through confrontation' (*phrad 'joms*) refers to knowing [the conceptual thoughts] to be empty, as if they were snow falling on hot rocks. 'Cutting them off' (*rjes bcad*) refers to the cutting of afflictions; for this you should examine from what [source] they arise."

182 Padmasambhava, *Padma bka' thang*, p. 644; Toussaint, *Le Dict de Padma*, p. 435.

183 These lines of Padampa Sanggyé were recited to Milarepa and are found in the latter's *Mgur 'bum*, p. 757; Chang, *The Hundred Thousand Songs of Milarepa*, p. 610.

184 Mi la ras pa, *Mgur 'bum*, p. 316; Chang, *The Hundred Thousand Songs of Milarepa*, pp. 151–52. The last word in the first line of Khöntön's text should read *thong* instead of *thob*.

185 The central channel and the two side channels are part of the subtle physiology of the human body. The three channels meet at certain points in the body, the forehead being one of these places.

186 'Brom ston Rgyal ba'i 'byung gnas (1005–64), the chief disciple of Atiśa and the founder of the Kadam (Bka' gdams) school of Tibetan Buddhism.

187 The text's *rtogs pa* has been emended to *rtog pa*.

188 One of the eighty-four *mahāsiddhas* of India and the teacher of the great Indian sage Nāropa. He lived at the end of the tenth and beginning of the eleventh century.

189 The exact verse is also quoted twice by Dagpo Trashi Namgyel; Takpo Tashi Namgyal, trans., *Mahāmudrā*, 192, 221. Despite searching for the lines, I have not been able to find them in the works attributed to Tilopa in the Bstan 'gyur. It appears that Lhalungpa encountered a similar problem, since he too does not mention their source. Similar (though not identical) lines are found in Tilopa's *Dohakośa*, *Do ha mdzod*, Sde dge Bstan 'gyur. Toh. no. 2281, Rgyud *shi*, fols. 136a–137b. For example: "Reality is not something scholars can fathom. *Kye ho!* It is only the object of those individuals who

take pleasure in serving the master. This is Tilopa's proclamation. Whatever is an object of thought can never be the ultimate." Similar lines are attributed to Tilopa by the Third Karmapa Rangjung Dorjé (Rang byung rdo rje, 1284–1339) in his *Sku gsum ngo sprod*, Gsung 'bum (Zi ling: Mtshur phu mkhan po lo yag bkra shis, 2006), vol. 11 (a), fol. 9a: "Mahāmudrā cannot be taught. For example, what supports space, and what does space support? Likewise, Mahāmudrā, one's own mind, has no support. Just relax into the uncontrived primordial state." An almost identical line to the last line cited by Khöntön Rinpoché is also found in Saraha, *Dohakośopadeśa, Mi zad pa'i gter mdzod man ngag gi glu*, Sde dge Bstan 'gyur, Toh. no. 2264, Rgyud *zhi*, fol. 29b: *rang la rang gis de nyid mtshon te ltos*.

190 Götsangpa Gönpo Dorjé (Rgod tshang pa Mgon po rdo rje, 1129–58), a famous early master of the Kagyü school. He was a disciple of the first Drugchen Rinpoché, Tsangpa Gyaré ('Brug chen Gtsang pa rgya ras, 1161–1211), and of Wönré Darma Senggé (Dbon ras Dar ma seng ge, 1177/78–1237). He was also a teacher of Yang Gönpa, mentioned and quoted above.

191 I have yet to find the lines in the works of Götsangpa, but the same verse is quoted by Zhabdrung Mingyur Dorjé, *Phyag chen las 'phros pa'i rang lan*, pp. 559–60.

192 The *Gnas lugs mdzod* of the great Nyingma master Longchen Rabjampa (Klong chen rab 'byams pa, 1308–64). These lines are found in chapter 4. See Longchen Rabjam, *The Precious Treasury of the Way of Abiding*, ed. and trans. by Richard Barron (Junction City, CA: Padma Publishing, 1998), pp. 54–55, 217–18. See also Gregory Alexander Hillis, "The Rhetoric of Naturalness: A Critical Study of the Gnas lugs mdzod" (Ph.D. dissertation, University of Virginia, 2003), part II, p. 148.

193 Lingrepa Pema Dorjé (Gling ras pa Pad ma rdo rje, 1128–88), a student of Pagmodrupa Dorjé Gyelpo (Phag mo gru pa Rdo rje rgyal po, 1110–70) and the teacher of Tsangpa Gyaré, the Drugpa Kagyü founder.

194 This is part of a song sung by Marpa when he first met his Indian teacher Nāropa. It is found in the *Ocean of Songs of the Kagyü Masters* (*Bka' brgyud mgur mtsho*); 'Bri gung skyabs mgon che tshang Dkon mchog bstan 'dzin 'phrin las, *Bka' brgyud rin po che'i mgur mtsho ye shes byin 'bebs* (Dehradun, India: D. Tsondu Senghe Yorey Tshang, 1991), pp. 63–64. See also Nālandā Translation Committee, *The Rain of Wisdom* (Boulder: Shambhala, 1980), p. 131

195 *Gnas* = *gnas pa*.

196 *'Gyu* = *'gyu ba*.

197 *Rig* = *rig pa*.

198 As the author states early on in the text, these are the Great Middle Way, the Great Seal (Mahāmudrā), and the Great Perfection (Dzogchen). Given that the subject being discussed here is the view common to all three, it cannot be the unique view of the seminal essence.

199 Saraha, *Dohakośa*, Sde dge Bstan 'gyur, Toh. no. 2224, Rgyud *wi*, fol. 73a. These lines are also cited by Zang Rinpoché in *Bla ma zhang, Theg pa che chung gi grub mtha'i skor las; Rnal 'byor lam gyi rim pa nyi ma'i snang ba*, in Gsung 'bum (Kathmandu: Gam-po-pa Library, 2004), vol. 2, p. 746; and also in his *Tai lo chos drug*, fol. 4a.

200 The lines are found in the famous prayer requested of Guru Padmasambhava by Nam mkha'i snying po, the "Le'u bdun ma" (Prayer in Seven Parts); see Jamgon Mipham, *White Lotus: An Explanation of the Seven-Line Prayer to Guru Padmasambhava*, trans. by Padmakara Translation Group (Boston: Shambhala, 2007).

201 Padmasambhava, *Padma bka' thang*, p. 645; Toussaint, *Le Dict de Padma*, p. 435.

202 These same lines from Longchenpa's *Treasury of Reality* were quoted above.

203 *Gnas pa*.

204 *Nyams myong*.

205 *Rtogs pa*.

206 *Cig car ba*.

207 *Thod rgal ba*.

208 *Rim gyis pa*.

209 The exposition of the three types of individuals that follows is based chiefly on a work of the Kagyü master Zhang Rinpoché. But similar explanations are also found in the Nyingma tradition. For example, Zhabdrung Mingyur Dorjé, *Gzhi lam 'bras bu'i gnad bsdus rig pa'i me long* (*Mirror of Awareness: A Brief Presentation of Some Points Related to the Basis, Path, and Result*), Gsung 'bum, fols. 341–43, states: "The *instantaneous type* realizes that all sights and sounds are not true things…and when they have reached decisiveness regarding the meaning of that realization, they obtain the result. For the *skipping type*, various experiences, both higher ones and lower ones, arise; nonetheless, so long as they exert themselves in their practice, after some time they are able to meld the equipoise and aftermath states. *Gradualists* first have understanding; in the middle, they have experiences; and in the end, realizations are gradually born. This leads to their attaining unchangeable confidence in the

nature of their realizations, and from that they actualize the result through irreversible mastery of the effulgence (*rtsal*) of great gnosis."

210   The line can also be translated, "Then experiences arise as certainty."

211   This is a procedure in which the master points out the nature of mind to the disciple.

212   In what follows Khöntön Rinpoché will distinguish among three distinct states: equipoise (*mnyam bzhag*), the aftermath consciousness (*rjes shes*), and the aftermath state (*rjes thob*). This is somewhat different from the more common bipartite division into equipoise and aftermath (or post-equipoise) states; see, for example, Takpo Tashi Namgyal, *Mahāmudrā*, pp. 285–92. But the threefold division is known in other texts of the Mahāmudrā tradition. For example, in a text based on a teaching of Yang Gönpa, the *Khor yug ma'i khrid dpe*, *Collected Writings (Gsuṅ 'bum) of Rgyal-ba yang-dgon-pa rgyal-mtshan-dpal* (Thimpu: Tango Monastic Community, 1984), vol. 1: pp. 200–201, we find:

> As regards *equipoise*, according to the texts of the great Lord Yang Gönpa, equipoise is accepted as having four qualities: clarity (*gsal ba*), lucidity (*dangs pa*), subtlety (*phra ba*), and nonconceptuality (*mi rtog pa*). The lucidity (*dangs ma*) of equipoise refers to the fact that it does not fall into object appearances (*yul snang*).
>
> The chief point of equipoise, according to Zhang Rinpoché, is as follows:
>
>> To say that something is equipoise or aftermath
>> is to say that one is standing up or sitting down.
>
> By which he means that so long as one is not disconnected from the recollection of self-clarity (*rang gsal*) or from the recollection of union (*zung 'jug*)—that is, so long as there is no discontinuity between any of the four activities one engages in—there is no wavering from the state of equipoise.
>
> The *aftermath state* (*rjes thob*) refers to naked immersion into the self-aware state by continuously recollecting [the equipoise] from the second and third moments [after one arises from the meditation].
>
> The *aftermath consciousness* (*rjes shes*) refers to entering into a more coarse state (*phya la la 'gro ba*) without recollection and grasping (*dran 'dzin med par*).
>
> Hence, those who engage in practice without discontinuity, no

matter which of these may arise, have purified a grasping at "equipoise" and "aftermath." And when this has occured, no matter which of the six or eight groups of objects appear to the five doors [of the senses], one remains steadfast within a practice whose nature is unified. That is the single taste of the manifold (*du ma ro gcig*). It is called the *single taste of the manifold* because manifold appearances are blended into a unified practice. The unified essence has gained contol over the manifold appearances, and one experiences various incongruous magical signs wherein a single appearance or non-appearance becomes many, and where the many become one; and all the phenomena of saṃsāra and nirvāṇa that may appear become aids to one's practice, without having to practice one thing and abandon another, or to negate one thing and affirm another. Whatever arises in awareness is just allowed to be.

In the end, one reaches the state of the result, and having become one with the mind of all the buddhas, having become the great Vajradhara, whose nature is the four bodies and five gnoses, all actions and activities become equalized. This is what it means to reach the state of final buddhahood.

213 The Tibetan text reads *rngas ma*, which can mean "cushion" or, more likely, "harvest." This translation is, however, tentative.

214 Bye tshang pa Rin chen dpal 'byor. He is listed in a lineage list in the Fifth Dalai Lama's *Record of Teachings Received* (*Thob yig*) as a student of Drenchog Sanggyé Tsöndrü (Dran mchog Sangs rgyas brtson 'grus) and as the teacher of Gyelsé Sanggyé Dechen (Rgyal sras Sangs rgyas bde chen). The latter was in turn the teacher of Khöntön Rinpoché's own teacher Nyida Sanggyé. Sanggyé Tsöndrü, Chetsangpa's teacher, is mentioned in the final verses of the present text as the chief source of the teachings contained in this very work. A text on Dzogchen by a certain Bye tshang pa has been translated by James Low in *Simply Being: Texts in the Dzogchen Tradition* (Vajra Publications, 1998), but this work is unavailable to me.

215 In the text we find *nyams* (experience), but given the context, one wonders whether this might not perhaps better be emended to read *mnyam bzhag* (equipoise).

216 When Gampopa was asked what it meant to unite equipoise and post-equipoise periods, he said: "It means to be able to engage in all actions without losing the single-pointedness of equipoise, or, in the post-equipoise stage,

to have conceptual thoughts act as an aid [to one's development]." Sgam po pa, *Rje dags po'i zhal gdams*, in Gsung 'bum (Delhi: Shashin, 1976), vol. 1 (*ka*), p. 360.

217   All three lines are found in the *Songs of the Kagyü Masters*, but the first two lines occur much later in the Marpa chapter, and are actually attributed by Marpa to Maitripa. The last line quoted here is found in Marpa's song to Nāropa mentioned above, which occurs earlier in the Marpa chapter. In the *Bka' brgyud mgur mtsho* version, the earlier lines read: "The illusory machinations of the outer and inner [world] I realized as the unborn Mahāmudrā" (*phyi nang sgyu ma'i 'khrul 'khor 'di/ skye med phyag rgya chen por rtogs*); 'Bri gung skyabs mgon, *Bka' brgyud mgur mtsho*, p. 63. The first two lines quoted here, as just mentioned, occur later in this same chapter. In the *Mgur mtsho* version, the last line of the triplet has "Dharma body" (*dharmakāya*) instead of "Mahāmudrā": "And I realized them to be the unborn Dharma body" (*skye med chos kyi sku ru rtogs*). 'Bri gung skyabs mgon, *Bka' brgyud mgur mtsho*, p. 100. Nālandā Translation Committee, *The Rain of Wisdom*, pp. 131, 153.

218   As the Nyingmapa master Zhigpo Dütsi (Zhig po bdud rtsi, 1149–99) states in his *Rdzogs pa chen po'i man ngag* (*Instructions on the Great Perfection*), Bka' ma shin tu rgyas pa (Chengdu: Kaḥ thog mkhan po 'jam dbyangs, 1999), pp. 135–37: "Wisdom is to relax the body, speech, and mind. [p. 136] Don't be bothered with the tracks of the past, what came before. Don't anticipate the future. Don't follow the objects of the five [senses] in the present. Just let consciousness operate without judgment. As [the master] A ro states:

> Without bothering about the tracks of what came before, give up on thoughts of the past.
> Without anticipating what lies ahead, cut the ties of attachment.
> Without grasping at anything in the in-between, look into the sphere of space.
> These are the essential instructions on uniting the three times.

"And the *Great Space* (*Nam mkha' che*) states:

> The three times are one. They are not different.
> Everything arises primordially: no before, no after.
> Because the Dharma body pervades [everything], it is all one.
> Thus, the essence is the great vastness.

"By settling into such [a state, the mind] becomes clear and nonconceptual.

This is the clarity of a consciousness that is lucid and grasps at nothing. Since this is the message of the buddhas of the three times, yogis [p. 137] should practice it."

219 These lines are found almost verbatim in Bla ma zhang, *Slob dpon shāk ye sku mched la gsungs pa'i khrid yig gsal ba'i sgron me*, found in the "Nyams len sgom khrid" section of his Gsung 'bum (Kathmandu: Gam-po-pa Library, 2004), vol. 3 (*ga*), fol. 11b. Zhig po bdud rtsi, *Man ngag nor bu 'jug sgo gsum pa*, Bka' ma shin tu rgyas pa (Chengdu: Kaḥ thog mnkhan po 'jam dbyangs, 1999), vol. 7, pp. 38–39: "The practice of the view consists of focusing on whatever affliction or conceptual thoughts arise without giving free rein to them. By so doing you allow them to be self-liberated into the lack of intrinsic existence, the unborn state. Those [afflictions and conceptual thoughts] are nothing but mind anyway. They appear on their own and are self-liberated without obstruction. Because their arising and their lack of intrinsic existence are simultaneous, they are nondualistically self-liberated. In brief, whatever afflictions or conceptual thoughts arise, you focus on them without giving free rein to them, and then, becoming self-liberated without any difference in their arising and ceasing, they simply vanish. That is why the *Meditation on Mind* (*Sems bsgom*) states:

No matter what conceptual signs are operating,
   if you understand that those very conceptual thoughts are reality,
   it becomes unnecessary to meditate on anything except the
      dharmadhātu,
   and it is unnecessary to counteract them, or to apply antidotes.

"This is the practice of the view. It is extremely important."

220 Following the passage cited in the previous note, Zhigpo Dütsi continues: "When the mind is clear and lacks conceptual thoughts, a consciousness that is clear and that does not grasp [at anything] arises. When that consciousness arises in a clear and lucid manner, it is called *meditation*" (p. 40).

221 *Dus tshod gcig.* The translation is uncertain, although generally there are said to be twelve *dus tshod* in one day. The expression is also found in Bla ma zhang, *Phyag rgya chen po dbu snyung ma*, in the "Nyams len sgom khrid" section of his Gsung 'bum (Kathmandu: Gam-po-pa Library, 2004), vol. 3 (*ga*), pp. 391–92: "Do not follow the traces of the many evanescent conceptual thoughts. Rather, allow them to settle into this vivid awareness (*rig pa hrig ge ba*). Settle and be relaxed.... By meditating in this way again and again, when within one *dus tshod* you have identified the conceptualizations and had a full

realization of them as groundless and devoid of foundation, all conceptions are liberated into their natural state."

222 Sgam po Zla 'od gzhon nu (1079–1153), that is, the Kagyü master Gampopa, the famous disciple of the great yogi Milarepa.

223 Similar sentiments—that conceptualizations are of the very nature of the Dharma body—are found throughout the works of Gampopa; e.g., in his *Rnam rtogs don dam gyi ngo sprod*. See Trungram Gyatrul Rinpoche Sherpa, "Gampopa, the Monk and the Yogi: His Life and Teachings" (Ph.D. dissertation, Harvard University, 2004), passim.

224 This analogy is already found in Bla ma zhang, *Tai lo chos drug*, fol. 5b: *de las g.yengs pa med pa bu gcig shi ba'i ma lta bu*. The line might perhaps also be read "Like a dying mother's [longing for] her only son."

225 Śāntideva, *Bodhicaryāvatāra*, 5:33, Sde dge Bstan 'gyur, Toh. no. 3871, Dbu ma *la*, fol. 11b.

226 *Rnal 'byor drug pa*. The lines are not found in the *Rnal 'byor yan lag drug pa = Yogaṣaḍaṅga* of Śavari, Toh. no. 1375, Rgyud *wi*, fols. 251a–b.

227 I have emended the text's *rtog pa* to read *rtogs pa* here.

228 I have not found this verse in the writings of Saraha, but it is well known in the Tibetan tradition. See, e.g., Khenpo Könchog Gyaltsen, *The Garland of Mahāmudrā Practices*, trans. and ed. by Katherine Rogers (Ithaca, NY: Snow Lion Publications, 1986), p. 85.

229 The editors of the Tibetan text suggest emending *gzings* (ship) to *gzeb* (cage). But there is a famous metaphor found in Mahāmudrā texts of the raven that is allowed to fly off from a ship in the middle of the ocean. The raven flies for some time, thinking that it is free. But with nowhere to land, it must eventually return to the ship. Likewise, if mind is set free, with nowhere to go, it eventually returns to its own natural state.

230 Bla ma zhang, *Phyag rgya chen po thog babs* (*Mahāmudrā Thunderbolt*), in the "Nyams len sgom khrid" section of his Gsung 'bum, vol. 3 (*ga*), p. 461.

231 Padmasambhava, *Padma bka' thang*, p. 645; Toussaint, *Le Dict de Padma*, p. 435.

232 These three lines are found, though not in the same order, in *Padma bka' thang*, pp. 644–45; Toussaint, *Le Dict de Padma*, p. 435.

233 This sentence is less than clear in the original, and the translation is tentative.

234 The translation of the phrase *rang la rang phar* [= '*bar*?] *so ma shor* is tentative.

235 '*Das rjes*. Two texts are known under this name in Atiyoga section of the

Collected Tantras of the Nyingma (Rnying ma rgyud 'bum). In this case the lines are from the one called *Rig 'dzin gyi 'das rjes* (*The Testament of the Awareness Holder*), Rnying ma rgyud 'bum, Mtshams brag edition, Tb. 348, vol. 14, fols. 263b–264a.

236   *Kun tu bzang po klong drug pa'i rgyud*, a tantra found in the Atiyoga section of the Rnying ma rgyud 'bum, Mtshams brag ed., Tb. 296, fol. 214a. In that edition, the first line in Khöntön Rinpoché's text is actually the first line of the verse that precedes this one. In the Rnying ma rgyud 'bum edition, the first line of the verse quoted here reads instead *sgom du yod pa'i sems nyid la*: "Within the nature of mind that is in a state of meditation."

237   *Brtag gnyis.*

238   *Hevajra Tantra*, 8:36; Rāmśaṅkar Tripāṭhī, ed., *Hevajratantram* (Sarnath: Central Institute for Higher Tibetan Studies, 2001), 91: *nānyena kathyate sahajaṃ na kasminnāpi labhyate/ ātmanā jñayate puṇyād gurūparvopasevayā/.* The entire verse is also quoted in Tilopa, *De kho na nyid bzhi pa'i man ngag gsal ba'i sgron ma*, Sde dge Bstan 'gyur, Toh. no. 1242, Rgyud *nya*, fol. 160b. It is also quoted by Gampopa in a reply to a question of Pagmodrupa in *Rje phag mo gru pa'i zhu lan*, vol. *ta* of the Sde dge edition of *Dwags po gsung 'bum*. The first line is quoted by Dagpo Trashi Namgyel; Lhalungpa, trans., *Mahāmudrā*, pp. 221, 483.

239   Gampopa was known for stressing the importance of devotion to a qualified spiritual master as the source of all realization. In his *Reply to Pagmodrupa's Questions* (*Rje phag mo gru pa'u zhu lan*), he goes so far as to say that the combination of the disciple's devotion and master's blessing is the *white panacea* (*dkar po gcig thub*) that cures all suffering.

240   The text's *skos phor* has been emended to read *rkos phor*.

241   Phag mo gru pa Rdo rje rgyal po was a student of Gampopa, and founder of the monastery of Ensa Til (Dben sa thel), the main seat of the Pagdru Kagyü school.

242   As in the case of a previous verse of Tilopa cited above, I have not been able to find this verse in the works attributed to Tilopa in the Bstan 'gyur.

243   Rgod tshang pa. Two figures are known under this name. One is Rgod tshang pa Sna tshog rang grol (1494–1570), a student of Gtsang smyon He ru ka (1452–1507) and of Padma gling pa (1450–1521); a master of both the Kagyü and Nyingma lineages, he was important in the transmission of the oral lineage of Rechungpa (Ras chung snyan brgyud). The other is Rgod tshang pa Mgon po rdo rje (1189–1258), mentioned earlier, a student of Tsangpa Gyaré and of Wönré Darma Senggé. Only further investigation

will allow us to determine which of these two figures our author is referencing, although see the following note.

244 A similar passage from Götsangpa is quoted by Yang Gönpa in Yang dgon pa, *Phyag rgya chen po lhan cig skyes sbyor gyis thos chos*, Gsung 'bum (Thimpu: Tango Monastic Community, 1984), vol. 1 (*ka*), p. 237: "To meditate on the Mahāmudrā, rest in the uncontrived, primordial ground. Let thoughts and concepts vanish on their own. Remain carefree in regard to appearances; let the variety [that exists in the world] act as an aid [to your practice]."

245 Saraha, *Dohakośacaryāgīti*, *Do ha mdzod zhes bya ba'i spyod pa'i glu*, Sde dge Bstan 'gyur, Toh no. 2263, Rgyud *zhi*, fols. 26b–27a, which varies slightly from the version in our text. The canonical version reads: *ji ltar rlung gis rgyab pas mi g.yo ba'i/ chu la g.yo bas rba rlabs rnams su 'gyur/ de ltar rgyal pos mda' bsnun snang ba yang/ gcig nyid na yang sna tshogs byed/ ji ltar rmongs pas bzlog nas bltas pa yis/ mar me gcig nyid gnyis su snang ba ltar/ de la blta bya lta byed gnyis med la/ kye ma blo ni gnyis kyi dngos por snang/.*

246 If the treasure is discovered, then it leads to the eradication of poverty (realization), but if it is not found, then the poor person remains poverty-stricken (nonrealization).

247 *Hevajratantra*, 4:69; Tripāṭhi ed., *Hevajratantram*, p. 188: *sattvā buddhā eva kiṃ tu āgantukamalāvṛtāḥ/ tasyāpakarṣaṇāt sattvā buddhā eva na saṃ-śayaḥ/.* The end of the Sanskrit verse simply adds, "of this there is no doubt." The passage is also cited by Dagpo Trashi Namgyel; see Takpo Tashi Namgyal, *Mahāmudrā*, pp. 219–20 and 483.

248 *Doha*. The Sanskrit is used here. This particular song is found in Saraha's *Dohakośa*; see Schaeffer, *Dreaming the Great Brahmin*, p. 112.

249 The lines quoted here appear to be a pastiche of three different verses in Milarepa's songs; *Mi la'i mgur 'bum*, pp. 637–38. The relevant verses read: *lta ba yin par nges kyis rang gi sems la ltos/ sems las gzhan du lta ba btsal ba na/ kyod kyi nor 'tsho 'dra'o ang ge lha rje ston pa ba/... 'bras bu yin par nges kyis sems la nges shes skyed/ thog med 'bras bu gzhan nas btsal ba na/ spal ba gnam du mchongs pa 'dra'o ang ge lha rje ston pa ba/ bla ma rin par nges kyis rang gi sems la dris/ sems las gzhan pa'i bla ma btsal pa na/ de yi rang sems spangs pa 'dra'o ang ge lha rje ston pa ba/*; Chang, *The Hundred Thousand Songs of Milarepa*, pp. 476–77. The lines are also found in 'Bri gung skyabs mgon, *Bka' brgyud mgur mtsho*, pp. 208–9; Nālanda Translation Committee, *Rain of Wisdom*, pp. 221–22; and also in Gampopa, *The Jewel Ornament of Liberation*, trans. by Gyaltsen and Chödron, p. 314.

250 Our text's *Mda' ka ye shes* has been emended to read *'Da' ka ye shes.* *Ātajñānasūtra*, Sde dge Bka' 'gyur, Mdo sde *tha*, Toh. no. 122, fol. 153a.

251 *Uttaratantra*, one of the five works of Maitreya and arguably the most important exoteric text for understanding the doctrine of buddha nature (*tathāgatagarbha*).

252 Rkang 'khyam pa could tentatively be translated as "Footloose"; the reference is unclear.

253 Gser gling pa Chos kyi grags pa or Dharmakīrti (b. tenth century), a teacher of the great Indian scholar-saint Atiśa. Tradition tells us Serlingpa lived in Sumatra.

254 The lines are almost certainly from Serlingpa's advice to Atiśa, advice on how to subdue barbarian lands, the *Bla ma gser gling pa jo bo la mtha' 'khob 'dul ba'i chos su gnang ba*, preserved in Dkon mchog rgyal mtshan, *Blo sbyong brgya rtsa*, p. 137. The lines found in the latter text, however, are somewhat different from those found in Khöntön Rinpoché's work. In Dkon mchog rgyal mtshan's compendium they read: *rgyangs kyis bskyur ba'i chos gcig yin/* [four additional lines are found at this point, and then] *log rtser log na rtsa rtser ltos/ shig ge shig la 'bol ler zhog/ de nas mi 'ching grol bar 'gyur/.*

255 The text's *chod* has been emended to *mchong*.

256 *Glegs bam rin po che* = *The Book of Kadam* (*Bka' gdams glegs bam*). The lines are found in the latter work exactly as cited in Khöntönpa's text; see Thupten Jinpa, trans., *The Book of Kadam: The Core Texts* (Boston: Wisdom Publications, 2008), p. 463, see also pp. 271–72.

257 The verse is cited in Takpo Tashi Namgyal, *Mahāmudrā*, p. 268.

258 Sha ba ri pa (tenth century) "the hunter" or "mountain man," one of the great Indian adepts (*mahāsiddhas*). In the traditional hagiographical accounts, he is considered a student of Nāgārjuna and a teacher of Maitripa. Śavari is also credited with having taught the famous Kālacakra six-part yoga to Tibetan disciples.

259 The lines are not found in Śavari's collection of vajra songs in the Bstan 'gyur, *Phyag rgya chen po rdo rje'i glu*, Toh. no. 2287, Rgyud *zhi*, fols. 150a–152b; nor are they found in his famous *Yogaṣaḍaṅga*, Toh. no. 1375, Rgyud *pa*, fols. 251a–b. I have also searched in vain for these lines in various minor liturgical works attributed to Śavari in the canon. The two lines, however, are quoted in Dagpo Trashi Namgyel's text, and have been located by Lhalungpa (see Takpo Tashi Namgyal, *Mahāmudrā*, p. 486, reference to 275F Śavari). Lhalungpa, however, does not give the name of the text, and because he used a version of the canon unavailable to me, I have been unable to check this reference.

260 'Jig rten mgon po (1143–1217), the founder of the Drigung Kagyü school ('Bri gung bka' brgyud), who built the monastery of Drigung Til ('Bri gung mthil).

261 Spyan mnga' ba has been emended to read Spyan snga ba. This is most likely one of Jigten Gönpo's successors to the throne of Drigung Til (see previous note): perhaps 'Bri gung spyan snga ba Shes rab 'byung gnas (1187–1241) or 'Bri gung spyan snga Grags pa 'byung gnas (1175–1255).

262 The text may be corrupt at this point, and the translation is uncertain.

263 The Golden Isle is a metaphor for unity and lack of differentiation. The Indian mahāsiddha Śavari says, "If you go to the Golden Isle, you will find no earth and stones, even if you search for them"; *Phyag rgya chen po rdo rje'i glu*, Sde dge Bstan 'gyur, Toh. no. 2287, Rgyud shi, fol. 152b: *gser gling phyin nas sa rdo btsal mi rnyed*. Dilgo Khyentse Rinpoché explains the metaphor in this way: "The navigator who lands on the island made entirely of fine gold will not find a single nugget, no matter how hard he searches. [Likewise,] we must understand that all of the qualities of Buddha have always existed in our being"; "Dilgo Khyentse Rimpoche on Dzogchen Meditation," at http://www.keithdowman.net/dzogchen/khyentse_meditation.htm. Anne Klein and Tenzin Wangyal, *Unbounded Wholeness: Dzogchen, Bon, and the Logic of the Nonconceptual* (Oxford: Oxford University Press, 2006), p. 94, also suggest that the Golden Isle is a place where there are no stones, and hence that it is a place of uniformity. The Golden Isle is mentioned in a variety of other texts. In the song the ḍākinī Niguma sings to Khyungpo Neljor, for example, we find the following lines:

> Son, the moment you realize the lack of intrinsic existence
> of attachment, hatred, and the various conceptual thoughts
> that cast you into the ocean of saṃsāra,
> everything becomes the Golden Isle.

'khor ba'i rgya mtshor bskyur na yi/ chags sdang rtog pa sna tshogs 'di/ rang bzhin med par rtogs tsa na/ thams cad gser gling yin no bu/; Nicole Riggs, *Like an Illusion: Lives of the Shangpa Kagyu Masters* (Eugene, OR: Dharma Clouds, 2001), p. 289.

In a tantra of the Nyingma school, the *Klong chen rab 'byams rgyal po'i rgyud* (Rnying ma rgyud 'bum, Mtshams brag ed., Tb. 238, chap. 27, p. 543), we also find the following lines:

> Because it is devoid of the extremes of arising and destruction,

It is devoid of anything to do: the great expanse, the state of space.
And because there is nothing to be cleared up, no acceptance or
 rejection,
It is a spacious expanse, like the Golden Isle.

264 In other words, since this is the final nature of all phenomena, there is nothing greater than Mahāmudrā. Hence, it is the highest nature, that which
"seals."

265 *Hevajra Tantra*, 5:1; Rāmśaṅkar Tripāṭhī, ed., *Hevajratantram*, p. 51: *nāsti
rūpaṃ na draṣṭā ca na śabdo nāpi śrtotā ca/ na gandho nāpi ghrātā ca na raso
cāpi rasakaḥ/ na sparśā nāpi spraṣṭā ca/.* According to the Sanskrit, the first
line should read, "There is no form and no one to see it."

266 *Ratnaguṇasaṃcayagāthā*, *Sdud pa* = *Shes rab kyi pha rol tu phyin pa sdud pa'i
tshig su bcad pa.* The lines quoted here are exactly as found in Gung thang
Dkon mchog bstan pa'i sgron me's *Annotations, 'Phags pa shes rab kyi pha rol
tu phyin pa sdud pa mchan dang bcas pa* (*The Condensed Verses of the Perfection of Wisdom with Notes*); Asian Classics Input Project (ACIP) digital file,
S0902, fol. 9a.

267 The verse is found in Tilopa's instructions to Nāropa called the *Mahāmudropadeśa, Phyag rgya chen po man ngag* (*Instructions on Mahamudra*), Sde
dge Bstan 'gyur, Toh. no. 2303, Rgyud *zhi*, fol. 243a. Per the Tengyur version,
the *rtsod chod* in Khöntön's text has been emended to read *rtsad chod*.

268 The verse is found in the *Collected Songs of the Kagyü Masters*; 'Bri gung
skyabs mgon, *Bka' brgyud mgur tsho*, p. 192. Nālandā Translation Committee, *Rain of Wisdom*, p. 210.

269 Atiśa, *Caryāsaṃgrahapradīpa, Spyod pa bsdus pa'i sgron ma* (*The Lamp: A
Compendium of Practices*), Sde dge Bstan 'gyur, Toh. no. 3960, Dbu ma *khi*,
fol. 313a.

270 *Rtsal.*

271 In Rgod tshang pa Mgon po rdo rje, *Rje rgod tshang pu'i dum bca' zhal gdams
dang rnal 'byor bzhi'i zhig tig*, Gsung 'bum, (Thimpu: Tango Monastic Community, 1981), vol. 3 (*ga*), fols. 5a–b, Götsangpa mentions such practices for
each of the four yogas. For the yoga of single-pointedness, it is the *armor and
effort* (*go cha dang brtson 'grus*). For the yoga of nonelaboration it is *faith and
devotion* (*mos gus*). For the yoga of the single taste, it is *love and compassion*
(*byams rnying rje*). And for the yoga of no-meditation, it is the *exhaustion of
mind and the exhaustion of dharma* (*blo zad chos zad*). See also Tselé Natsog Rangdröl, the "Enhancement" section from his *Lamp of Mahāmudrā,*

translated in Urgyen Tulku et al., *Quintessential Dzogchen* (Boudanath: Rangjung Yeshe Publications, 2006), chap 32.

272 One of the three stages of the Mahāmudrā yoga of single-pointedness. This will be explained below.

273 That things are like illusions, dreams, echoes, magical spirit cities, hallucinations, mirages, optical illusions, and reflections in a mirror.

274 *Method* (*thabs*) is one of the two accumulations amassed by bodhisattvas on their way to buddhahood. The other is *wisdom* (*shes rab*). The lines are found in Atiśa, *Mahāyānapathasādhanavarṇasaṃgraha*, *Theg pa chen po'i lam gyi sgrub thabs yi ger bsdus pa* (*A Brief Treatise on the Method of Practicing the Mahāyāna Path*), Sde dge Bstan 'gyur, Toh. no. 3954, Dbu ma *khi*, fol. 302b, where the text reads:

> Having meditated on calm abiding, one meditates on insight.
> Once you have accomplished insight,
> during the periods following the state of equipoise,
> accustom yourself to seeing all phenomena
> as being like the eight examples of illusory things.
> In such a way should you chiefly cultivate
> the view subsequent [to equipoise] and train in method.

zhi gnas la brten lhag mthong bsgom/ lhag mthong grub par gyur pa yis/ mnyam gzhag langs pa'i dus dag tu/ sgyu ma'i dpe brgyad lta bur ni/ chos kun lta ba goms byas pas/ rjes kyis rtogs pa sbyang ba dang/ thabs la slob pa gtso bor bya/.

275 Rgyal sras rin po che, literally, Precious Child of the Conqueror. A variety of masters are known by this title, and only further investigation will allow us to determine who is being cited here. Given that the stanza is directed to a "Maniwa," the verse is almost certainly written by a Tibetan.

276 The three poisons are anger, desire, and delusion.

277 The four yogas are the yoga of single-pointed concentration, of nonelaboration, of the single taste, and of no-meditation. These will be explained in what follows. They are explained at length in a variety of Mahāmudrā works like Bla ma zhang's *Rnal 'byor lam gyi rim pa*, pp. 746ff., and in his *Rnal 'byor bzhi'i rnam bzhag* (*Setting Forth the Four Yogas*), Gsung 'bum, vol. 3 (*ga*), fols. 568–82. They are also explained in Yang dgon pa's *Ri chos kyi rnal 'byor bzhi pa phyag rgya chen po snying po don gyi gter mdzod*, Gsung 'bum, vol. 1 (*ka*), pp. 247–284, and in Rgod tshangs pa Mgon po rdo rje, *Rgyal ba rgod tshangs pa'i gsung sgros rnal 'byor bzhi gsum bcu gnyis zin bris rgyal ba u rgyan pas mdzad pa*, in Gsung 'bum (Thimpu: Tango Monastic Community, 1981), vol. 3 (*ga*),

fols. 1a–12b. The latter text was actually composed by U rgyan pa Rin chen dpal (1229/30–1309) in the form of notes based on Götsangpa's teachings. I believe this text to be a major influence on Khöntön Rinpoché's thought and on the present work. According to Yang Gönpa (p. 291), the doctrine of the four yogas originates as a distinct system from of the realizations of Gampopa (*phyir rnal 'byor bzhi pa'i rim pa 'di rnams/ rje sgam po pa'i rtogs chos yin*), though Yang Gönpa then goes on to show canonical foundations for the system by quoting, e.g., the *Tantra of Inconceivable Secrets* (*Acintyaguhyanirdeśa, Gsang ba bsam gyis mi khyab pa'i rgyud*).

Such terminology (single-pointedness, nonelaboration, single taste, equal taste, no-meditation, and so on) is, of course, found in a variety of Indian Mahāmudrā works. A "four-part Mahāmudrā" (*phyag rgya chen po bzhi*) is mentioned in one of the works attributed to Saraha, the *Kāyakośāmṛtavajragīti, Sku'i mdzod 'chi med rdo rje'i glu*, Sde dge bstan 'gyur, Toh. no. 2269, Rgyud *zhi*, fols. 214–27. Saraha's system, however, is quite different from the one described here. For Saraha, the four parts are: (1) the part that realizes the meaning of unborn (*skye med don rtogs pa yi yan lag*), (2) the part on the unity of the two truths (*bden pa gnyis tha mi dad kyi yan lag*), (3) the part where appearances are directly realized as unborn, and where one ceases to grasp at thought (*snang ba skye med thug phrad nyid du rtogs/ dran pa gzung du med pa'i yan lag*), and (4) the transcendence of mind, devoid of emptiness as a condition and devoid of thought, where there is nothing to be abandoned or accomplished (*stong pa rkyen dang dran med blo las 'das/ dngos po dgag sgrub med pa'i yan lag*).

278   The five paths are the paths of (1) accumulation, (2) preparation, (3) seeing, (4) meditation, and (5) no more learning.

279   It is unclear what our author means here by "ascertainment consciousness." Lama Zhang states that "During the period of the yoga of single-pointedness, no ascertainment consciousness is generated, and that is why [this yoga] is troubled by appearances." Bla ma zhang, *Rnal 'byor bzhi'i gnas lugs* (*The Nature of the Four Yogas*), Gsung 'bum, vol. 3 (ga), p. 595: *rtse gcig gi rnal 'byor gyi dus na nges shes ma skyes pas snang bas gnod do*.

280   Bla ma zhang, *Rnal 'byor bzhi'i gnas lugs*, p. 595: "What is the difference between *śamatha*, or mere stability, and the yoga of single-pointedness? During mere stability, the [mind's] steadiness is thick and conceptualization is blocked. During single-pointedness, conceptualization is not blocked; the steady samādhi is light, and the experience is totally lucid and clear. So there *is* a difference."

281 Bla ma zhang, *Rnal 'byor lam gyi rim pa*, pp. 749–50, states: "Having rid oneself of the notions of 'meditator' and 'what I meditate on,' all phenomena fully become the nature of the primordial state, the great bliss, the Dharma body. And when one has rid oneself of [notions of] accepting and rejecting [anything], and of all dualities, each and every phenomenon of both saṃsāra and nirvāṇa cease to have intrinsic existence. This is called the 'yoga of the river's stream' (*chu bo'i rgyun gyi rnal 'byor*). In this way, the yoga that unifies all things is called the 'attainment of the supreme accomplishment of Mahāmudrā.' It is also called 'mastery of the self-arisen gnosis (*rang byung ye shes*).'"

282 Rgod tshangs pa, *Rgyal ba rgod tshangs pa'i gsung sgros rnal 'byor bzhi gsum bcu gnyis zin bris*, fol. 12b: "What is the difference between the single taste and no-meditation? It is whether or not, in the aftermath, [things] are illusory-like; whether or not the thought of no-effort has been purified."

283 Various Tibetan scholars of Mahāmudrā and Dzogchen have sought to reconcile the stages of the path found in these two traditions with the classical path structure—the five paths and ten bodhisattva stages—found in exoteric Mahāyāna literature. Such reconciliations are found, for example, throughout the writings of the Kagyü master Götsangpa and in the works of the Nyingma master Longchen Rabjampa. For a translation of a passage of this kind in a work of Longchenpa, the *Gnyis ka'i yang yig nam mkha' klong chen*, see Tulku Thondup, *The Practice of Dzogchen* (Ithaca, NY: Snow Lion Publications, 1989), pp. 399–400.

284 These are the stages that bodhisattvas traverse during the path of meditation: (1) utter joy, (2) the stainless, (3) the shining, (4) the radiant, (5) the one that is difficult to overcome, (6) the actualized, (7) gone afar, (8) the immovable, (9) perfect intelligence, and (10) cloud of Dharma.

285 This is to say that the yoga of single-pointedness corresponds to the first two of the five paths: the paths of accumulation and preparation. Put another way, the yoga of single-pointedness corresponds to the stages of the path of the non-ārya bodhisattva, someone below the path of seeing who has not yet had a direct realization of emptiness. This is also the position of Rgod tshangs pa, *Rgyal ba rgod tshangs pa'i gsung sgros rnal 'byor bzhi gsum bcu gnyis zin bris*, fol. 3a: "What is the difference between single-pointedness and lack of elaborations? It is whether or not conceptions are or are not liberated into the Dharma body. Single-pointedness is a worldly (*lo ga'i = lo ka'i*) path. When conceptual thoughts are seen to be, or are liberated into, the Dharma body, this is called 'seeing the true nature of things, the lack of elaborations' (*spros*

bral ngo bo mthong ba). From the point of view of the mind of enlightenment (*sems bskyed*), it is the ultimate mind of enlightenment. From the point of view of the four empowerments, it is called 'obtaining the precious fourth or word empowerment.' From the point of view of the philosophers (*mtshan nyid ba*), it is called 'the path of seeing (*mthong lam*), the recognition to non-conceptual gnosis.'"

286 Gtsang pa rgya ras Ye shes rdor rje (1161–1211), the First Drugchen Rinpo-ché ('Brug chen rin po che), founder of the Drugpa Kagyü school. He established the monastery of Ralung (Rwa lung) in 1180.

287 This refers to the stages from the first bodhisattva bhūmi up to and including the seventh. The two explanations are presumably the classical one found in the literature on the bodhisattva paths and the special system explained in the four yogas of the Mahāmudrā.

288 Rgod tshangs pa, *Rje rgod tshang pa'i rnal 'byor bzhi'i zab 'brel* (sic), Gsung 'bum, vol. 3 (*ga*) part *ya*, fol. 2b, states, "According to the precious lord [i.e., according to Rgod tshang pa's teacher], the Lord Pagmodrupa divided each of the Lord Gampopa's four yogas into three, making a total of twelve, but he did not give any explanation. I have understood these in the following way." He then goes on to give his teacher's understanding of the twelve divisions. In the beginner's practice of single-pointedness, for example, "one abides on the true nature nonconceptually" (*ngo bo mi rtog par gnas pa*), although one wonders whether the text's *mi rtog par* ("nonconceptually") is an error, and should instead read *mi rtogs par* ("one abides *without realizing* the nature"). The middling practitioner of single-pointedness achieves "a more stable focus" (*gnas pa de brtan par song ba*). The most advanced one achieves "impure" extrasensory and magical powers (*zag bcas kyi mngon shes dang rdzu 'phrul ston nus pa 'byung*). Likewise, there are three stages to each of the other three yogas.

289 *Dpe'i 'od gsal*. This is an experience that arises as part of the completion stage of the highest yoga tantra in which the wind energies and their corresponding consciousnesses are dissolved into the central channel. It differs from the *actual clear light* insofar as it does not involve any sustained contemplation of reality.

290 Lha gzigs ras pa. His dates are unknown. He is the author of a Mahāmudrā text called *Dispelling Mental Darkness: A Teaching on the Coemergent Union Mahāmudrā* (*Phyag rgya chen mo lhan cig skyes sbyor gyi khrid yig ma rig mun sel*), which unfortunately does not seem to have survived, but the text is known to us from the fact that it is mentioned in Akhu Rinpoché's list of rare works.

291 Sa skya paṇḍita Kun dga' rgyal mtshan (1182–1251). Sapen is known as a critic of certain Tibetan elaborations of Mahāmudrā, and this is what Khöntön Rinpoché now discusses.

292 Sa paṇ, *Sdom gsum rab dbye*, vv. 403–4; translated by Jared Rhoton in Sakya Pandita, *A Clear Differentiation of the Three Codes*, pp. 149, 316. A line is missing from Khöntön Rinpoché's text: *gal te mdo dang rgyud sde las*; it is the second line in this verse and has been inserted in square brackets.

293 In all mental states that are "direct perceptions"—including yogic direct perception—there is a waning, or absence, of dualistic appearances, appearances of the perceiving subject as distinct from the perceived object. Khöntönpa is here reiterating the well-accepted view that there is no waning of dualistic appearances (at least in regard to reality) during the first two paths (the paths of accumulation and preparation) and during the yoga of single-pointedness.

294 In other words, just as the goddess can be called "no-waist" not because she is actually without a waist, but metaphorically—i.e., because her waist is very thin—likewise, the first two stages of the yoga of no-meditation are called *no-meditation* not because they actually involve no meditation but because of their similarity to the stage of true no-meditation, the "great" stage of the yoga of no-meditation, the stage of buddhahood.

295 The position being portrayed here appears to be the one found in Sakya Paṇḍita's *Distinguishing the Three Vows*, vv. 254ff.; Sakya Pandita, *A Clear Differentiation*, pp. 129, 308.

> There is no difference in the way the view is explained
> in the Perfection [of Wisdom] and tantric [scriptures]. (254)
> If there were, then there would be a view
> superior to the lack of elaborations [taught] in the Perfection
> [of Wisdom scriptures].
> This would mean that [the latter] view would actually possess
> elaborations.
> But when something is [truly] the lack of elaborations, it cannot be
> differentiated [into higher and lower]. (255)

pha rol phyin dang gsang sngags la/ lta ba'i dbye ba bshad pa med/ (254) *pha rol phyin pa'i spros bral las/ lhag pa'i lta ba yod na ni/ lta de spros pa can du 'gyur/ spros bral yin na khyad par med/* (255). For Dagpo Trashi Namgyel's response to Sakya Paṇḍita's critique of Mahāmudrā, see Takpo Tashi Namgyal, *Mahāmudrā*, pp. 241–42.

296 These lines are found in Sapaṇ's *Distinguishing the Three Vows*, v. 254. See previous note.

297 If so, then this would of course contradict Khöntön Rinpoché's assertion here, given that he believes that only the first yoga, the yoga of single-pointedness, can be found among ordinary beings, beings below the path of seeing.

298 Three schools of the Kagyü: the Karma Kagyü (Kar ma bka' brgyud), founded by the First Karmapa, Düsum Khyenpa (Dus gsum mkhyen pa, 1110–93); the Drugpa Kagyü ('Brug pa bka' brgyud), founded by Tsangpa Gyaré; and the Gampo Kagyü, founded by Gampopa, sometimes also called Dagpo Kagyü (Dwags po bka' bgryud). Today the latter is not usually considered a separate subschool but rather the tradition that gave rise to several of the other Kagyü schools.

299 *Nyan sa* = *Śrāvakabhūmi*, written by the Indian scholar-saint Asaṅga (third–fourth centuries C.E.).

300 *Kun bstus* = *Abhidharmasamuccaya*, written by Asaṅga.

301 *Sgom rim* = *Bhāvanākrama*, written by the Indian scholar-saint Kamalaśīla (ninth century).

302 Maitreya, *Abhisamayālaṃkāra*, *Mngon rtogs rgyan*, Sde dge Bstan 'gyur, Toh. no. 3786, Shes phyin *ka*, fol. 2b.

303 Nāgārjuna, *Yuktiṣāṣṭikā*, *Rigs pa drug bcu pa*, verse 60. The text has been edited and translated in Lindtner, *Nagarjuniana*; the passage cited here is found on pp. 118–19.

304 *Lam shes.*

305 *Gzhi'i lta ba.*

306 Dpal ldan zla ba = Candrakīrti (seventh century), an Indian scholar whose *Introduction to the Middle Way* (*Madhyamakāvatāra*) came to be considered the most authoritative expression of the Middle Way philosophy in post thirteenth-century Tibet.

307 *Madhyamakāvatāra*, *Dbu ma la 'jug pa*, 6:80; La Vallée Poussin, *Madhyamakāvatāra*, p. 174; Huntington, *Emptiness of Emptiness*, p. 167.

308 These lines are not actually contained in the *Madhyamakāvatāra*. Khöntön Rinpoché is stating that they are implied by the previous lines.

309 Nāgārjuna, *Ratnāvalī*, *Rin chen phreng ba*, 2:18; edited in Michael Hahn, *Nāgārjuna's Ratnāvalī*, Indica et Tibetica Band 1, vol. 1 (Bonn: Indica et Tibetica Verlag, 1982), p. 47.

310 *Madhyamakāvatāra*, *Dbu ma la 'jug pa*, 6:79; La Vallée Poussin, *Madhyamakāvatāra*, p. 174; Huntington, *Emptiness of Emptiness*, pp. 166–67.

311 *De kho no nyid bcu pa* = *Tattvadaśaka*; Sde dge Bstan 'gyur, Toh. no. 2236, Rgyud *wi*, fol. 113a.

312 Mdo sde pa = Sautrāntika.

313 Bye brag smra ba = Vaibhāṣika.

314 I have yet to locate these lines. A similar claim is found in Maitripa's *Explaining Non-Abiding*; *Rab tu mi gnas pa gsal bar ston pa*, Sde dge Toh. no. 2235, Rgyud *wi*, fol. 112b.

315 Grangs can = Vaiśeṣika, one of the classical schools of Indian philosophy.

316 Candrakīrti, *Catuḥśatakaṭīkā*, *Bzhi brgya pa'i 'grel pa*, a commentary on Āryadeva's *Four Hundred Stanzas*; Sde dge Bstan 'gyur, Toh. no. 3865, Dbu ma *ya*, fol. 190b.

317 Buddhapālita (470–550), the earliest Indian commentator on the *Mūlamadhyamakakārikā* of Nāgārjuna.

318 Buddhapālita, *Buddhapālitamadhyamakavṛtti*, Dbu ma rtsa ba'i grel pa buddha pā li ta, Sde dge Bstan 'gyur, Toh. no. 3842, Dbu ma *tsa*, fol. 198a. The canonical version varies just slightly from the citation here.

319 These lines from the *Bodhicaryāvatāra* (from 9:140) were cited above. See note 162.

320 Āryadeva, *Catuḥśataka*, *Bzhi brgya pa*, 14:23cd; Karen Lang, ed. and trans., *Āryadeva's Catuḥśataka*, Indiske Studier 7 (Copenhagen: Akademisk Forlag, 1986), pp. 134–35.

321 Candrakīrti, *Catuḥśatakaṭīkā*, *Bzhi brgya pa'i 'grel pa*, fol. 220b.

322 *Sgom rim tha ma*; the third of the three *Bhāvanākramas* written by the Indian master Kamalaśīla; Sde dge Bstan 'gyur, Toh. no. 3917, Dbu ma *ki*, fol. 62b.

323 *Sgom rim bar ma*; the second of the three *Bhāvanākramas* of Kamalaśīla. See previous note. Sde dge Bstan 'gyur, Toh. no. 3916, Dbu ma *ki*, fol. 49a. These lines are also cited by Dagpo Trashi Namgyel; see Takpo Tashi Namgyal, *Mahāmudrā*, 34.

324 Tsong kha pa, *Byang chub lam rim che ba* (Mtsho sngon: Mi rigs dpe skrun khang, 1985), pp. 768–69; *The Great Treatise of the Stages of the Path to Enlightenment*, trans. by Joshua Cutler et al., vol. 3 (Ithaca, NY: Snow Lion Publications, 2000–2004), p. 325.

325 The three major schools of the "later propagation of the doctrine": the Kagyü, Sakya, and Kadam/Gelug.

326 Vimalamitra was an eighth-century Indian Buddhist master who went to Tibet and whose teachings became the core of one of the most important Dzogchen lineages.

327 Sangs rgyas brtson 'grus (b. fifteenth century), a student of Kun dga' nyi ma (b. fifteenth century), who was in turn a student of the famous saint Thang stong rgyal po (1361–1485). Sanggyé Tsöndrü was an important figure in the transmission of the Northern Treasures of the Nyingma school. He was the

teacher of Padma sangs rgyas, who was in turn the teacher of Khöntönpa's own teacher, Nyi zla sangs rgyas. Unfortunately, none of Sanggyé Tsöndrü's writings seem to have survived.

328 Sprul sku ba 'Phrin las lhun grub.

329 See page 37 in the biography of Khöntön Rinpoché earlier in this volume.

330 Sbyor drug = Ṣaḍaṅgayoga, the most important practice of the completion stage of the Kālacakra tantra. One of the most important lineages of the practice of the six-limbed yoga in Tibet was that systematized by the Indian adept Śavari mentioned earlier.

331 The core meditation system of the Kagyü tradition. The six Dharmas are inner heat, illusory body, clear light, dream yoga, intermediate state, and transference of consciousness.

332 Dpal 'byor bsod nams lhun grub (b. fifteenth century), one of Khöntön Peljor Lhündrub's main teachers at Sera Monastery; see the biography.

333 This list appears in the 'Khon ston entry in the Tibetan Buddhist Resource Center website TBRC resource code P 647; http://tbrc.org/#library_person_Object-P647.

334 Here abbreviated *Shing rta*; see note 1.

335 This text apparently survives. See above. Akhu Rinpoché (MHTL 11219) gives an alternative title: *Skyabs 'gro'i khrid yig yid ches gsum ldan.*

336 According to TBRC, the *Bod rig pa'i tshig mdzod chen mo* (p. 2329), states that this work was composed in 1614. This is probably based on a reference found in Jamyang Zhepa; see *Tibetan Chronological Tables*, p. 219.

337 This, of course, is the work translated in this book. We know the date of composition from evidence internal to the text. *Shing rta* only discusses the text in the context of a discussion of the teachings Khöntön Rinpoché gave in the year 1621.

338 The text, which is extant (TBRC W1CZ1111), states that it was written at Pabongkha—which means that it was most likely written sometime after 1619, when Khöntönpa moved to the hermitage. But no exact date is given in the colophon.

339 The work is extant. It was written at Pabongkha. Although the colophon does not give the exact date of composition, Khöntönpa mentions his year of composition several times in the book (pp. 61, 120, 121, 130). That year is *rab byung bcu gcig pa'i sa 'brug pa*; that is, 1628.

340 The Fifth Dalai Lama, *Shing rta*, fol. 35b, explains that this and the next work were controversial treatises that were seen "by some as words that had The'u rang demons as their source and by others as sheer arrogance." But the Dalai

Lama goes on to defend the works, seeing them as examples of the clairvoyance of his master, as practices that had many precedents in Tibetan history, and, empirically, as *true* based on the political events that happened after 1629. Note that in the TBRC list, these two works are considered one.

341 The comment is found in the *Bka' rgyud gser phreng*, in *Ta'i si tu pa kun mkhyen chos kyi 'byung gnas bstan pa'i nyin byed kyi bka' 'bum* (Delhi: Palpung Sungrab Nyamso Khang, 1990), vol. na, p. 360. I have Tashi Tsering of the Amnye Machen Institute to thank for this reference. Zhamar Rinpoché believed and publicly proclaimed that Tshangs dbyangs rgya mtsho was the true reincarnation of the Fifth Dalai Lama (*rje tshangs dbyang rgya mtsho ni lnga pa'i yang srid yin*), for which he was fined five hundred *dngul srang* by the Mongolian ruler. The monks of Sera and Drepung, he states, helped him to pay this fine through their generous gifts, suggesting that these Gelug monks, too, were opposed to Lhazang's candidate (*dngul srang lnga brgya bsgrub dgos byung yang ser 'bras kyi grwa tshang rnams nas gnang cha ches pas bde blags tu 'grig pa byung*). The statement also suggests that in the early eighteenth century, when the Zhamarpa was writing, Khöntönpa's reincarnations had yet to be identified with the Changkya line, as would happen later.

342 See Smith, *Among Tibetan Texts*, p. 161; *Ming mdzod*, pp. 526–27.

343 In some enumerations, Mkhas grub Grags pa 'od zer is considered the First Changkya Lama, in which case all of the following would be increased by one.

344 See Smith, *Among Tibetan Texts*, p. 164; and *Ming mdzod*, pp. 527–29.

345 On his life and works, see Xiangyun Wang, "Tibetan Buddhism at the Court of Qing: The Life and Work of lCang-skya Rol-pa'i-rdo rje" (Ph.D. dissertation, Harvard University, 1995). See also Smith, *Among Tibetan Texts*, chap. 11, and p. 170; and *Ming mdzod*, pp. 529–30.

346 For this and the next two figures in the lineage, the different dates correspond to those suggested, respectively, by Smith (*Among Tibetan Texts*, p. 146) and by the authors of the Wikipedia entry, "lCang-skya Khutukhtu" at http://en.wikipedia.org/wiki/LCang-skya_Khutukhtu. See Smith, *Among Tibetan Texts*, p. 308n472.

347 See Kevin Garratt, "Biography by Installment: Tibetan Language Reportage on the Lives of Reincarnate Lamas, 1995–99," in P. Christian Klieger, ed., *Tibet, Self, and the Tibetan Diaspora: Voices of Difference*, Proceedings of the International Association of Tibetan Studies 2000 (Leiden: Brill, 2002), p. 89.

Bibliography

Ahmad, Zahiruddin. *Sino-Tibetan Relations in the Seventeenth Century*. Rome: Istituto Italiano per il Medio ed Estremo Oriente, 1970.

Ary, Elijah Sacvan. "Logic, Lives and Lineage: Jetsun Chökyi Gyaltsen's Ascension and the *Secret Biography of Khedrup Geleg Pelzang*." Ph.D. dissertation, Harvard University, 2007.

Ātajñānasūtra. *'Phags pa 'Da' ka ye shes zhes bya ba theg pa chen po'i mdo*. Sde dge Bka' 'gyur, Toh. no. 122, Mdo sde *tha*, fols. 153a–b.

Atiśa. *Caryāsaṃgrahapradīpa. Spyod pa bsdus pa'i sgron ma*. Sde dge Bstan 'gyur, Toh. no. 3960, Dbu ma *khi*, fols. 312b–313a.

———. *Mahāyānapathasādhanavarṇasaṃgraha. Theg pa chen po'i lam gyi sgrub thabs yi ger bsdus pa*, Sde dge Bstan 'gyur, Toh. no. 3954, Dbu ma *khi*, fols. 299a–302b.

Bdud 'joms 'Jigs bral ye shes rdo rje. *Gangs jongs rgyal bstan yongs rdzogs kyi phyi mo snga 'gyur rdo rje theg pa'i bstan pa rin po che ji ltar byung ba'i tshul dag cing gsal bar brjod pa lha dbang g.yul las rgyal ba'i rnga bo che'i sgra dbyangs*. Bound book; no bibliographical information other than the date, 1990.

Bla ma zhang. *Phyag rgya chen po dbu snyung ma*. In Gsung 'bum, vol. 3 (*ga*), pp. 391–93. Kathmandu: Gam-po-pa Library, 2004.

———. *Phyag rgya chen po lam khyer*. In Gsung 'bum, vol. 3 (*ga*), pp. 513–27. Kathmandu: Gam-po-pa Library, 2004.

———. *Phyag rgya chen po thog babs*. In Gsung 'bum, vol. 3 (*ga*), pp. 456–90. Kathmandu: Gam-po-pa Library, 2004.

———. *Rnal 'byor bzhi'i gnas lugs*. In Gsung 'bum, vol. 3 (*ga*), pp. 588–98. Kathmandu: Gam-po-pa Library, 2004.

———. *Rnal 'byor bzhi'i rnam bzhag*. In Gsung 'bum, vol. 3 (*ga*), pp. 568–82. Kathmandu: Gam-po-pa Library, 2004.

———. *Rnal 'byor lam gyi rim pa*. In Gsung 'bum, vol. 3 (*ga*), pp. 693–760. Kathmandu: Gam-po-pa Library, 2004.

———. *Slob dpon shāk ye sku mched la gsungs pa'i khrid yig gsal ba'i sgron me*. In Gsung 'bum, vol. 3 (*ga*), pp. 357–68. Kathmandu: Gam-po-pa Library, 2004.

———. *Tai lo chos drug*. In Gsung 'bum, vol. 3 (*ga*), pp. 344–57. Kathmandu: Gam-po-pa Library, 2004.

———. *Theg pa che chung gi grub mtha'i skor las / Rnal 'byor lam gyi rim pa nyi ma'i snang ba*. In Gsung 'bum, vol. 2, pp. 693–760. Kathmandu: Gam-po-pa Library, 2004.

Brauen, Martin, ed. *The Dalai Lamas: A Visual History*. Chicago: Serindia, 2005.

'Bri gung skyabs mgon che tshang dkon mchog bstan 'dzin 'phrin las. *Bka' brgyud rin po che'i mgur mtsho ye shes byin 'bebs*. Dehradun: D. Tsondu Senghe Yorey Tshang, 1991.

Brunnhölz, Karl. *Straight from the Heart: Buddhist Pith Instructions*. Ithaca, NY: Snow Lion Publications, 2007.

Bstan 'dzin lung rtogs nyi ma. *Rdozgs chen chos byung chen mo*. Beijing: Krung go'i bod rig pa dpe skrun khang, 2004.

Buddhapālita. *Buddhapālitamadhyamakavṛtti. Dbu ma rtsa ba'i grel pa buddha pā li ta*. Sde dge Bstan 'gyur, Toh. no. 3842, Dbu ma *tsa*, fols. 158b–181a.

Cabezón, José I. "On the *Grwa pa rin chen pa'i rtsod len* of Paṇ chen blo bzang chos rgyan." *Asiatische Studien/Études Asiatiques* 46.4 (1995): 643–69.

———. *The Hermitages of Sera*. Charlottesville: Tibetan and Himalayan Digital Library, 2006. Online publication available at: http://www.thlib.org/places/monasteries/sera/hermitages/pdf/sera_hermitages.pdf.

Cabezón, José Ignacio, and Geshe Lobsang Dargyay. *Freedom from Extremes: Gorampa's "Distinguishing the Views" and the Polemics of Emptiness*. Boston: Wisdom Publications, 2006.

Candrakīrti. *Catuḥśatakaṭīkā. Bzhi brgya pa'i 'grel pa*. Sde dge Bstan 'gyur, Toh. no. 3865, Dbu ma *ya*, fols. 30b–239a.

———. *Madhyamakāvatāra. Dbu ma la 'jug pa*. Sde dge bstan 'gyur, Toh. no. 3861, Dbu ma *'a*, fols. 201b–219a.

Chandra, Lokesh. *Materials for a History of Tibetan Literature* (MHTL). Kyoto: Rinsen Book Co., 1981.

Chang, Garma C. C., trans. *The Hundred Thousand Songs of Milarepa*. Boston: Shambhala, 1999.

Chattopadhyaya, Alaka, and Sanjit Kumar Sadhukhan, trans. *Tibetan Chronological Tables of Jam-dbyaṅs bźad-pa and Sum-pa mkhan-po*. Sarnath: Central Institute of Higher Tibetan Studies, 1993.

Cozort, Daniel. *Highest Yoga Tantra*. Ithaca, NY: Snow Lion Publications, 2005.

[Dalai Lama V] Ngag dbang blo bzang rgya mtsho. *Khyab bdag 'khor lo'i dbang phyug dpal 'byor lhun grub kyi rnam thar skal bzang dad pa'i shing rta*. In Gsung 'bum, vol. *nya*, pp. 609–96. Gangtok: Sikkim Research Institute of Tibetology, 1991–95.

Dalai Lama, His Holiness the. "Concerning Dholgyal with reference to the views of past masters and other related matters." October 1977. Online at http://www.dalailama.com/page.155.htm.

Dalai Lama, His Holiness the, and Alexander Berzin. *The Gelug/Kagyü Tradition of Mahamudra*. Ithaca, NY: Snow Lion Publications, 1997.

Dalai Lama, His Holiness the, Tsong-kha-pa, and Jeffrey Hopkins. *Tantra in Tibet*. Ithaca, NY: Snow Lion Publications, 1987.

Daśabhūmikasūtra. Sa bcu pa'i mdo. Sde dge Bka' 'gyur, Toh. no. 44, Phal chen *kha*, chap. 26.

Dilgo Khyentse Rinpoche. "Dilgo Khyentse Rimpoche on Dzogchen Meditation," at http://www.keithdowman.net/dzogchen/khyentse_meditation.htm.

Dkon mchog rgyal mtshan. *Blo sbyong brgya rtsa dang dkar chag gdungs sel zla ba*. Dharamsala: Shes rig par khang, 1973.

Dkon mchog 'jigs med dbang po. *Rje btsun thams cad mkhyen pa lcang skya rol pa'i rdo rje'i khrung rab kyi phreng ba gtam du brjod pa ngo mtshar dad pa'i ljong shing*, in *The Collected Works of Dkon-mchog 'jigs-med dbang-po*. Gaden Sung-rab Minyam Gyunphel Series 22, vol. 2. New Delhi: Ngawang Gelek Demo, 1971.

Dorje, Gyurme. "The *Guhyagarbhatattvaviniścayamahātantra* and Its XIVth Century Tibetan Commentary: Phyogs bcu mun sel." Ph.D. dissertation, University of London, 1987.

Dudjom Rinpoche. *The Nyingma School of Tibetan Buddhism: Its Fundamentals and History*, 2nd ed. Trans. by Gyurme Dorje and Matthew Kapstein. Boston: Wisdom Publications, 2002.

Dwags po Bkra shis rnam rgyal. *Phyag chen sgom rim zla ba'i 'od zer*. Mtsho sngon: Mi rigs dpe skrung khang, 2001.

Gampopa. *The Jewel Ornament of Liberation*. Trans. by Khenpo Konchog Gyaltsen and Ani K. Trinlay Chödron. Ithaca, NY: Snow Lion Publications, 1998.

Garratt, Kevin. "Biography by Installment: Tibetan Language Reportage on the Lives of Reincarnate Lamas, 1995–99." In P. Christian Klieger, ed., *Tibet, Self, and the Tibetan Diaspora: Voices of Difference*, Proceedings of the International Association of Tibetan Studies 2000, pp. 57–104. Leiden: Brill, 2002.

Gser gling pa. *Sems dpa'i rim pa* (*Stages of the Heroic Mind*), preserved in a collection of mind-training texts by Dkon mchog rgyal mtshan, *Blo sbyong brgya rtsa dang dkar chag gdungs sel zla ba*, pp. 126–36. Dharamsala: Shes rig par khang, 1973.

———— . *Bla ma gser gling pa jo bo la mtha' 'khob 'dul ba'i chos su gnang ba*, preserved in Dkon mchog rgyal mtshan, *Blo sbyong brgya rtsa*, pp. 136–37. Dharamsala: Shes rig par khang, 1973.

Gu ru Bkra shis ngag dbang blo gros. *Gu bkra'i chos 'byung*. Mtsho sngon: Krung go'i bod kyi shes rig dpe skrung khang, 1990.

Gung thang Dkon mchog bstan pa'i sgron me. *'Phags pa shes rab kyi pha rol tu phyin pa sdud pa mchan dang bcas pa*. Asian Classics Input Project CD-Rom, digital file S0902.

Gyatrul Rinpoche. *The Generation Stage in Buddhist Tantra*. Ithaca, NY: Snow Lion Publications, 1996.

Hadano, H. "A Historical Study in the Problems Concerning the Diffusion of Tantric Buddhism in India: Advayavajra, alias Mñaḥ-bdag-Maitripā." In T. Ishizu et al., eds., *Religious Studies in Japan*, pp. 287–99. Tokyo: Maruzen, 1959.

Hahn, Michael, ed. *Nāgārjuna's Ratnāvalī*. 2 vols. Indica et Tibetica 1. Bonn: Indica et Tibetica Verlag, 1982.

Harding, Sarah. *Machik's Complete Enlightenment*. Ithaca, NY: Snow Lion Publications, 2003.

Harrison, Paul. *The Tibetan Text of the Pratyutpanna-Buddha-Saṃmukhāvasthita-Samādhi Sūtra*. Studia Philologica Buddhica Monograph Series 1. Tokyo: The Reiyukai Library, 1978.

Hillis, Gregory Alexander. "The Rhetoric of Naturalness: A Critical Study of the Gnas lugs mdzod." Ph.D. dissertation, University of Virginia, 2003.

Huntington, C. W., with Geshé Namgyal Wangchen, trans. *The Emptiness of Emptiness*. Honolulu: University of Hawaii Press, 1989.

Jackson, Roger R. *Tantric Treasures: Three Collections of Mystical Verse from Buddhist India*. Oxford: Oxford University Press, 2004.

Jamgön Kongtrül. *Creation and Completion: Essential Points of Tantric Meditation*. Trans. by Sarah Harding with commentary by Khenchen Thrangu Rinpoche. Boston: Wisdom Publicatons, 1996.

Jamgon Mipham. *White Lotus: An Explanation of the Seven-Line Prayer to Guru Padmasambhava*. Trans. by the Padmakara Translation Group. Boston: Shambhala, 2007.

Jigme Lingpa, Patrul Rinpoche, and Getse Mahapandita. *Deity, Mantra, and Wisdom: The Development Stage in Tibetan Buddhist Tantra*. Trans. by the Dharmacakra Translation Committee. Ithaca, NY: Snow Lion Publications, 2006.

Jinpa, Thupten, trans. *Mind Training: The Great Collection*. Boston: Wisdom Publications, 2006.

———. *The Book of Kadam: The Core Texts*. Boston: Wisdom Publications, 2008.

Kamalaśīla. *Bhāvanākrama* [no. 1]. *Sgom pa'i rim pa*. Sde dge Bstan 'gyur, Toh. no. 3916, Dbu ma *ki*, fols. 42a–55b.

———. *Bhāvanākrama*. [no. 2]. *Sgom pa'i rim pa*. Sde dge Bstan 'gyur, Toh. no. 3917, Dbu ma *ki*, fols. 55b–68b.

———. *Bodhicittabhāvanā*. *Byang chub sems bsgom pa*. Sde dge Bstan 'gyur, Toh. no. 3913, Dbu ma *ki*, fols. 16b–19a.

Karmay, Samten. *Secret Visions of the Fifth Dalai Lama*. London: Serindia, 1999.

'Khon ston Dpal 'byor lhun grub. *Bde smon rnam bshad*. TBRC W1CZ1111. Scanned from a microfilm copy of a blockprint of unknown origin.

———. *Bstan bcos mngon par rtogs pa'i rgyan gyi 'grel ṭīk rnam bshad snying po'i rgyan gyi tshig don rab gsal*. No bibliographical information available. Mentioned at http://www.chibs.edu.tw/publication/chbj/02/chbj0205.htm.

———. *'Jam dpal gshin rje gshed skor gyi bla ma brgyud pa'i chos 'byung gdul bya'i re 'dod skong ba yid bzhin nor bu'i 'phreng ba*. Dharamsala: Library of Tibetan Works and Archives, 2005.

———. *Snyan brgyud yid bzhin nor bu lta ba spyi khyab tu ngo sprod pa'i khrid yig*. In *Sngags rdzogs dbu ma'i skor gyi dpe dkon thor bu'i rigs phyogs bsgrigs*. Bla rung sgar: Gser ljongs bla ma rung lnga rig nang bstan slob grwa chen mo, 2005.

Klein, Anne, and Tenzin Wangyal. *Unbounded Wholeness: Dzogchen, Bon, and the Logic of the Nonconceptual*. New York: Oxford University Press, 2006.

Klong chen rab byams pa. *Rzogs pa chen po bsam gtan ngal gso*. Reprint of the A 'dzom 'brug pa chos sgar xylographs, vol. 3: pp. 5–29. TBRC W23760, 1999.

Klong chen rab 'byams rgyal po'i rgyud. Rnying ma rgyud 'bum, Mtshams brag ed., Tb. 238, pp. 446–617.

Klong rdol bla ma. *Rgya bod du byon pa'i bstan 'dzin gyi skyes bu dam pa rnams kyi mtshan tho*. Asian Classics Input Project (ACIP) digital text, S6552E_T.

Ko shul Grags pa 'byung gnas and Rgyal ba Blo bzang mkhas grub. *Gangs can mkhas grub rim byon ming mdzod*. Chengdu: Kan su'u mi rigs dpe skrun khang, 1992.

Könchog Gyaltsen, Khenpo. *The Garland of Mahāmudrā Practices*. Trans. and ed. by Katherine Rogers. Ithaca, NY: Snow Lion Publications, 1986.

Køppl, Heidi I. *Establishing Appearances as Divine: Rongzom Chokyi Zangpo on Reasoning, Madhyamaka, and Purity*. Ithaca, NY: Snow Lion Publications, 2008.

Kun tu bzang po klong drug pa'i rgyud. Rnying ma rgyud 'bum, Mtshams brag ed., Tb. 296, vol. 12, pp. 394–467.

Lang, Karen, ed. and trans. *Āryadeva's Catuḥśataka*. Indiske Studier 7. Copenhagen: Akademisk Forlag, 1986.

"lCang-skya Khutukhtu." Online Wikipedia article at http://en.wikipedia.org/wiki/LCang-skya_Khutukhtu.

Lindtner, Christian, trans. and ed. *Nagarjuniana*. Copenhagen: Akademisk Forlag, 1982.

Lhalungpa, Lobsang P., trans. *The Life of Milarepa: A New Translation from the Tibetan*. New York: Penguin, 1992.

Longchen Rabjam. *The Precious Treasury of the Way of Abiding*. Trans. and ed. by Richard Baron. Junction City: Padma Publishing, 1998.

Low, James, trans. *Simply Being: Texts in the Dzogchen Tradition*. N.p.: Vajra Press, 1998.

Maitreya. *Abhisamayālaṃkāra. Mngon rtogs rgyan*. Sde dge Bstan 'gyur, Toh. no. 3786, Shes phyin *ka*, fols. 1a–13a.

Maitripa. *Explaining Non-Abiding; Rab tu mi gnas pa gsal bar ston pa*. Sde dge, Toh. no. 2235, Rgyud *wi*, fol. 112b.

Maitripa. *Tattvadaśaka. De kho no nyid bcu pa*. Sde dge Bka' 'gyur, Toh. no. 2236, Rgyud *wi*, fols. 112b–113a.

Martin, Dan, and Yael Bentor. *Tibetan Histories: A Bibliography of Tibetan-Language Historical Works*. London: Serindia, 1997.

Mdo dngags chos kyi rgya mtsho. Phyag rdzogs dbu gsum gyi lta ba'i dris lan mkhas pa'i zhal lung. In *Gsang sngags gsar rnying gi lta ba'i rnam bzhag legs bshad gces btus*, pp. 126–43. Dharamsala: Rnam rgyal grwa tshang shes yon lhan tshogs, 2009.

——— . *Snyan dgon sprul sku gsung rab pa'i gsung rtsom bces bsgrigs*. Zi ling: Mtsho sngon mi rigs dpe skrun khang, 1996.

Mdo dgongs 'dus. Sde dge bka' 'gyur, Toh. no. 829, Rnying rgyud *ka*, fols. 86b–290a.

Mi la ras pa. *Mi la'i mgur 'bum*. Gangtok: Sherab Gyaltsen, 1983. Reprint of the 1980 Mtsho sngon mi rigs dpe skrunb khang ed.

Nālandā Translation Committee, trans. *The Rain of Wisdom*. Boulder: Shambhala, 1980.

——— . *The Life of Marpa the Translator*. Boston: Shambhala, 1982.

Nges don Bstan 'dzin bzang po (Third Dzogchen Rinpoché). *Rdzogs pa chen po mkha' 'gro snying thig gi khrid yig thar lam bgrod byed shing rta bzang po*. Chengdu: Mi rigs dpe skrun khang, 1997.

Padmasambhava. *Padma bka' thang*. Chengdu: Mi rigs dpe skrung khang, 1996.

Paṇ chen Blo bzang chos kyi rgyal mtshan. *Dge ldan bka' brgyud rin po che'i bka' srol kyi phyag chen rtsa ba rgyal ba'i gzhung.* In Gsung 'bum, vol. 4 (*nga*), pp. 81–92. New Delhi: Mongolian Lama Gurudeva, 1973.

Patrul Rinpoche. *The Words of My Perfect Teacher.* Trans. by Padmakara Translation Group. San Francisco: HarperCollins, 1994.

Pha bong kha'i dkar chag. Hand-copy of a manuscript made available to Cabezón in Lhasa, 2004.

Rāmśaṅkar Tripāṭhī, ed. *Hevajratantram.* Sarnath: Central Institute for Higher Tibetan Studies, 2001.

Rang byung rdo rje (Third Karma pa). *Sku gsum ngo sprod.* In Gsung 'bum, vol. 11 (*a*), fols. 1a–10a. Zi ling: Mtshur phu mkhan po lo yag bkra shis, 2006.

Ratna gling pa. *Klong gsal snying thig gi brgyud pa'i lo rgyus.* In Gsung 'bum, vol. *da*, pp. 23–26. Darjeeling: Taklung Tsetrul Pema Wangyal, 1977–79.

Rgod tshang pa Mgon po rdo rje. *Rje rgod tshang pa'i dam bca' zhal gdams dang rnal 'byor bzhi'i zhig tig.* Gsung 'bum, vol. 3 (*ga*), part '*a*, fols. 1–6a. Thimpu: Tango Monastic Community, 1981.

———. *Rje rgod tshang pa'i rnal 'byor bzhi'i zab 'brel* (sic). Gsung 'bum, vol. 3 (*ga*) part *ya*, fols. 1a–8a. Thimpu: Tango Monastic Community, 1981.

———. *Rgyal ba rgod tshangs pa'i gsung sgros rnal 'byor bzhi gsum bcu gnyis zin bris rgyal ba u rgyan pas mdzad pa.* In Gsung 'bum, vol. 3 (*ga*), fols. 1a–12b. Thimpu: Tango Monastic Community, 1981.

Rig 'dzin gyi 'das rjes. Rnying ma rgyud 'bum, Mtshams brag edition, Tb. 348, vol. 14, fols. 263b–264a. Thimpu: National Library, Royal Government of Bhutan, 1982.

Riggs, Nicole. *Like an Illusion: Lives of the Shangpa Kagyu Masters.* Eugene, OR: Dharma Clouds, 2001.

Ringu Tulku. *The Ri-mé Philosophy of Jamgön Kongtrul the Great: A Study of the Buddhist Lineages of Tibet.* Boston: Shambhala, 2006.

Rtse le Sna tshogs rang grol. *Phyag rdzogs dbu gsum gyi lta sgom nyams len.* In Gsung 'bum, vol. 2, pp. 89–137. New Delhi: Sanji Dorje, 1974.

Sakya Pandita Kunga Gyaltshen. *A Clear Differentiation of the Three Codes: Essential Distinctions Among the Individual Liberation, Great Vehicle and Tantric Systems.* Trans. and ed. by Jared Rhoton and Victoria R. M. Scott. Albany: State University of New York Press, 2002.

Śāntideva. *Bodhicaryāvatāra. Byang chub sems dpa' spyod pa la 'jug pa.* Sde dge Bstan 'gyur, Toh. no. 3871, Dbu ma *la*, fols. 1–40a.

Saraha. *Dohakośa. Do ha mdzod kyi glu.* Sde dge Bstan 'gyur, Toh. no. 2224, Rgyud *wi*, fols. 70b–77a.

————. *Dohakośopadeśa. Mi zad pa'i gter mdzod man ngag gi glu.* Sde dge Bstan 'gyur, Toh. no. 2264, Rgyud *zhi*, fols. 28b–33b.

————. *Dohakośacaryāgīti. Do ha mdzod zhes bya ba'i spyod pa'i glu.* Sde dge Bstan 'gyur, Toh no. 2263, Rgyud *zhi*, fols. 26b–27a.

————. *Dohakośamahāmudropadeśa. Do ha mdzod ces bya ba phyag rgya chen po'i man ngag.* Sde dge Bstan 'gyur, Toh. no. 2273, Rgyud *shi*, fols. 122a–124a.

————. *Kāyakośāmṛtavajragīti. Sku'i mdzod 'chi med rdo rje'u glu.* Sde dge bstan 'gyur, Toh. no. 2269, Rgyud *zhi*, fols. 214–27.

Śavari. *Mahāmudrāvajragīti. Phyag rgya chen po rdo rje'i glu.* Sde dge Bstan 'gyur, Toh. no. 2287, Rgyud *zhi*, fols. 150a–152b.

————. *Yogaṣaḍaṅga. Rnal 'byor yan yag drug pa.* Sde dge Bstan 'gyur, Toh. no. 1375, Rgyud *pa*, fols. 251a–b.

Schaeffer, Kurtis. *Dreaming the Great Brahmin: Tibetan Traditions of the Buddhist Poet-Saint Saraha.* Oxford: Oxford University Press, 2005.

Sde srid Sangs rgyas rgya mtsho. *Dga' ldan chos 'byung bai ḍurya ser po.* Mtsho sngon: Mi rigs dpe skrung khang, 1991.

Sgam po pa. *Rje dags po'i zhal gdams.* Gsung 'bum, vol. 1 (*ka*), pp. 360–76. Delhi: Shashin, 1976.

Shaw, Miranda. *Passionate Enlightenment.* Princeton: Princeton University Press, 1994.

Si tu Chos kyi 'byung gnas. *Bka' brgyud gser phreng.* In *Ta'i si tu pa kun mkhyen chos kyi 'byung gnas bstan pa'i nyin byed kyi bka' 'bum*, vol. *na*. Delhi: Palpung Sungrab Nyamso Khang, 1990.

Smith, E. Gene. *Among Tibetan Texts: History and Literature of the Himalayan Plateau.* Boston: Wisdom Publications, 2001.

Sørensen, Per, and Guntram Hazod, with Tsering Gyalbo. *Rulers of the Celestial Plain: Ecclesiastical and Secular Hegemony in Medieval Tibet, a Study of Tshal Gung-thang.* Vienna: Verlag des Österreichischen Akademie der Wissenschaften, 2007.

Sweet, Michael J. "Mental Purification (Blo sbyong): A Native Tibetan Genre of Religious Literature." In José I. Cabezón and Roger R. Jackson, eds., *Tibetan Literature: Studies in Genre*, pp. 244–60. Ithaca, NY: Snow Lion Publications, 1996.

Takpo Tashi Namgyal. *Mahāmudrā: The Quintessence of Mind and Meditation.* Trans. by Lobsang P. Lhalungpa. Delhi: Motilal Banarsidass, 2001.

Tashi Densapa. "A Short Biography of 'Gro-mgon Chos-rgyal 'Phags-pa." *Bulletin of Tibetology*, New Series, 3 (1977): 7–14.

Tatz, Mark. "The Life of the Siddha Philosopher Maitri Gupta." *Journal of American Oriental Society* 107.4 (1987): 695–711.

Templeman, David, trans. and ed. *Tāranātha*. Dharamsala: Library of Tibetan Works and Archives, 1983.

Templeman, David, trans. and ed. *Tāranātha's Bka'.babs.bdun.ldan: The Seven Instruction Lineages by Jo.nang Tāranātha*. Dharamsala: Library of Tibetan Works and Archives, 1983.

Thondup, Tulku. *The Practice of Dzogchen*. Ithaca, NY: Snow Lion Publications, 1989.

Tilopa. *Dohakośa. Do ha mdzod*. Sde dge Bstan 'gyur, Toh. no. 2281, fols. 136a–137b.

——. *Mahāmudropadeśa. Phyag rgya chen po man ngag*. Sde dge Bstan 'gyur, Toh. no. 2303, Rgyud zhi, fols. 242b–244a.

——. *Tattvacaturupadeśaprasannadīpa. De kho na nyid bzhi pa'i man ngag gsal ba'i sgron ma*. Sde dge Bstan 'gyur, Toh. no. 1242, Rgyud nya, fols. 155b–162a.

Toussaint, Gustave-Charles. *Le Dict de Padma: Padma Thang Yig, Ms. de Litang*. Paris: Librairie Ernst Leroux, 1933.

Trungram Gyatrul Rinpoche Sherpa. "Gampopa, the Monk and the Yogi: His Life and Teachings." Ph.D. dissertation, Harvard University, 2004.

Tsong kha pa. *Byang chub lam rim che ba*. Mtsho sngon: Mi rigs dpe skrun, 1985.

——. *The Great Treatise on the Stages of the Path to Enlightenment*, 3 vols. Trans. by Joshua Cutler et al. Ithaca, NY: Snow Lion Publications, 2000–2004.

Urgyen Tulku, Erik Pema Kunsang, and Marcia Binder Schmidt. *Quintessential Dzogchen*. Boudanath: Rangjung Yeshe Publications, 2006.

La Vallée Poussin, Louis de, ed. *Madhyamakāvatāra par Candrakīrti*. St. Petersbourg: Imprimerie de l'Académie Impériale des Sciences, 1912.

Wang, Xiangyun. "Tibetan Buddhism at the Court of Qing: The Life and Work of lCang-skya Rol-pa'i-rdo rje." Ph.D. dissertation, Harvard University, 1995.

Williams, Paul. *Altruism and Reality: Studies in the Philosophy of the Bodhicaryāvatāra*. London: RoutledgeCurzon, 1997.

——. *Critical Concepts in Religious Studies*. London: Routledge, 2006.

Yang dgon pa Rgyal mtshan dpal. *Khor yug ma'i khrid dpe, Collected Writings (Gsuṅ 'bum) of Rgyal-ba yang-dgon-pa rgyal-mtshan-dpal*, vol. 1, pp. 285–92. Thimpu: Tango Monastic Community, 1984.

——. *Phyag rgya chen po lhan cig skyes sbyor gyis thon chos*. In Gsung 'bum, vol. 1 (ka), pp. 203–39. Thimpu: Tango Monastic Community, 1984.

——. *Ri chos kyi rnal 'byor bzhi pa phyag rgya chen po snying po don gyi gter mdzod*, Gsung 'bum, vol. 1 (ka), pp. 241–77. Thimpu: Tango Monastic Community, 1984.

Yeshe, Lama Thubten. *Becoming Vajrasattva: The Tantric Path of Purification*. 2nd ed. Ed. by Nicholas Ribush. Boston: Wisdom Publications, 2004.

Yongs 'dzin Ye shes rgyal mtshan. *Lam rim bla ma brgyud pa'i rnam thar.* Lhasa: Bod ljongs mi dmangs dpe skrun khang, 1990.

Zhabs drung Mi 'gyur rdo rje. *Phyag rgya chen po las 'phros pa'i rang lan rtsod pa'i mun sel.* In Gsung 'bum, pp. 521–603. New Delhi: Ngawang Topgay, 1981.

——— . *Gzhi lam 'bras bu'i gnad bsdus rig pa'i me long.* In Gsung 'bum, pp. 333–54. New Delhi: Ngawang Topgay, 1981.

Zhig po bdud rtsi. *Man ngag nor bu 'jug sgo gsum pa.* In Bka' ma shin tu rgyas pa, vol. 7, pp. 27–44. Chengdu: Kaḥ thog mkhan po 'jam dbyangs, 1999.

——— . *Rdzogs pa chen po'i man ngag.* In Bka' ma shin tu rgyas pa, vol. 7, pp. 133–38. Chengdu: Kaḥ thog mkhan po 'jam dbyangs, 1999.

Index

About the Authors

TENZIN GYATSO, the Fourteenth Dalai Lama, is renowned throughout the world as the embodiment of Buddhist wisdom and compassion. He was awarded the Nobel Peace Prize in 1989 and the Congressional Medal of Honor in 2007 for his tireless work for world peace and the liberation of Tibet. He lives in Dharamsala, India.

JOSÉ IGNACIO CABEZÓN is XIV Dalai Lama Professor of Tibetan Buddhism and Cultural Studies and Chair of the Religious Studies Department at the University of California Santa Barbara. The author of eleven books and dozens of scholarly articles, he was a Buddhist monk for ten years and studied at Sera Monastery in India from 1980 to 1985.

About Wisdom

WISDOM PUBLICATIONS, a nonprofit publisher, is dedicated to making available authentic works relating to Buddhism for the benefit of all. We publish books by ancient and modern masters in all traditions of Buddhism, translations of important texts, and original scholarship. Additionally, we offer books that explore East-West themes unfolding as traditional Buddhism encounters our modern culture in all its aspects. Our titles are published with the appreciation of Buddhism as a living philosophy, and with the special commitment to preserve and transmit important works from Buddhism's many traditions.

To learn more about Wisdom, or to browse books online, visit our website at www.wisdompubs.org.

You may request a copy of our catalog online or by writing to this address:

Wisdom Publications
199 Elm Street
Somerville, Massachusetts 02144 USA
Telephone: 617-776-7416
Fax: 617-776-7841
Email: info@wisdompubs.org
www.wisdompubs.org

Wisdom is a nonprofit, charitable 501(c)(3) organization affiliated with the Foundation for the Preservation of the Mahayana Tradition (FPMT).